WHERE DID JESUS DIE?

Where did Jesus Die?

The Messiah, son of Mary, was no more than a Messenger. All Messengers before him have passed away. And his mother was righteous. Both of them used to eat food. See how We explain the Signs for their good, and see how they are turned away.
(The Holy Quran 5:76)

by

J.D. Shams

Imam of the London Mosque 1936–1946

ISLAM INTERNATIONAL PUBLICATIONS LTD.

Where did Jesus Die?
written by Hazrat Maulana Jalal-ud-Din Shams[ra],
Imam of the London Mosque (1936–1946)

First published in UK, 1945
Eighth edition in UK, 1989
Ninth edition in UK, 1996
Tenth edition in UK, 2004
Eleventh edition in UK, 2014 (ISBN 1-85372-190-6)
Present Twelfth edition, printed in India, 2017

© Islam International Publications Ltd.

Published by
Nazarat Nashro Isha'at
Qadian 143516
District Gurdaspur (Punjab), India

Printed in India at
Fazl-e-Umar Printing Press
Qadian - 143516 (Punjab)

For further information please visit www.alislam.org.

ISBN 978-1-84880-892-8

CONTENTS

About the Author ix
Foreword to the First Edition xiii
Foreword to the Present Edition xvii
Introduction xix
Preface xxxv

Chapter One—Passages from the Gospels 3
Chapter Two—The Judgment 17
Chapter Three—The Story of the Resurrection 35
Chapter Four—Early Documentary Evidence 45
Chapter Five—Recent Discovery: Shroud
of Jesus 65
Chapter Six—Modern Medical Opinion 71
Chapter Seven—Did Jesus Ascend to Heaven? 79
Chapter Eight—Did Jesus Die on the Cross and
Ascend to Heaven? 89
Chapter Nine—Paganism and Paul 107
Chapter Ten—Redemption or Atonement 121
Chapter Eleven—Jesus Goes to India 139
Chapter Twelve—The Unknown Life of Jesus 175
Chapter Thirteen—Yus Asaph and Jesus 191
Chapter Fourteen—A Paramount Prophecy 205

Appendix to Sixth Edition 217
Appendix to Seventh Edition 223
Appendix to Twelfth Edition 231
Bibliography 237
Publisher's Note 243

The Tomb of Jesus—
Khanyar Street, Srinagar, Kashmir

According to the oral and written evidence of distinguished people in Srinagar, the occupant of the above tomb is a Prophet, Yus Asaf by name and also called Prince, who came to Kashmir some 1900 years ago. The author of the *Tarikh-i-Azami of Kashmir,* a historical work written some 200 years ago refers to this tomb as follows:

> The tomb next to that of Sayyed Nasr-ud-Din is generally known as that of a prophet who was sent to the inhabitants of Kashmir, and the place is known as the shrine of a prophet. He was a Prince who came to righteousness and devotion, he was made a prophet by God and was engaged in preaching to the Kashmiris. His name was Yus Asaf. (p. 82)

Yus Asaf in Hebrew means Jesus the Gatherer.

Hazrat Maulana Jalal-ud-Din Shams[ra]

ABOUT THE AUTHOR

Hazrat Maulana Jalal-ud-Din Shams[ra] was born in 1901 and was a companion of the Promised Messiah[as], Hazrat Mirza Ghulam Ahmad of Qadian. His father, Mian Imam-ud-Din Sekhwani[ra], his two paternal uncles, Mian Jamal-ud-Din Sekhwani[ra] and Mian Khair-ud-Din Sekhwani[ra], and his paternal grandfather, Muhammad Siddique Sekhwani[ra], were also companions of the Promised Messiah[as]—all of whom who were blessed to be included in the list of 313 Companions, along with their respective families.

Jamal-ud-Din, Khair-ud-Din, and Imam-ud-Din are recorded in the 'History of Ahmadiyyat' as the *Sekhwani Bradaraan* or *Sekhwani Brothers* after the town they lived in, Sekhwan, a few miles to the northwest of Qadian. The family used to pray in a mosque that was built by the father of the Promised Messiah[as] and they were well acquainted with the young Mirza Ghulam Ahmad[as] as he was growing up. When Ahmad[as] claimed to be the Mahdi and Messiah, the brothers and their families unanimously accepted his claim without question as they knew his truthful and virtuous character.

Growing up in this inspirational environment, the young Jalal-ud-Din Shams dedicated his life for the cause of Ahmadiyyat, and was trained to be a missionary by various companions of the Promised Messiah[as] including Hazrat Mirza Bashir-ud-Din Mahmud Ahmad[ra] and Hazrat Hafiz Raushan Ali[ra]. In 1925, Maulana Shams[ra] was dispatched to the Middle East where he founded the Ahmadiyya Muslim Community in Damascus, Syria. However, there he was viciously attacked from behind by a knife-wielding assailant and left for dead in a pool of blood. Fortunately, he was discovered by a neighbour and immediately taken to the hospital. The doctors' prognosis was grim and it was expected that he would soon die from the several knife wounds he sustained in his back. A telegram was sent to Hazrat Mirza Bashir-ud-Din Mahmud Ahmad, the Second Khalifah[ra], in Qadian to apprise him of the situation. He requested the Community to gather in Masjid Aqsa to collectively pray for Shams and another missionary in another locale. Miraculously, Shams started to heal within three days. Upon full recovery, the French authorities requested him to leave as they could not guarantee his protection.

Maulana Shams, under the guidance and direction of the Second Khalifah[ra], went to Palestine. There he frequented various centres of Muslim learning to preach the message of Ahmadiyyat. He established the Ahmadiyya Muslim Community in Kababir, Haifa (now in Israel) and laid the foundation of Mahmood Mosque. A street in Kababir is named after him. After delivering a lecture at the famous Dar-ul-Hikmah in Cairo, one of the Arab scholars stood up and questioned him where he received his knowledge. Shams replied that these are the teachings of the Mahdi. Astonished, the scholar then turned around to face the audience and said that this man is the Ibn Abbas of our generation.

Maulana Shams later returned to India in 1931; he married and had two children. He was appointed the Secretary of the All-India Kashmir Committee, of which the Second Khalifah[ra] was elected President and Sir Muhammad Iqbal was a member. He was then dispatched to England in 1936 to be the Imam of the London Mosque. As he did not know much English, he made an arrangement with a man in England to learn English from him in exchange for lessons in Arabic. Despite this initial language barrier, approximately sixty British citizens accepted Ahmadiyyat. He authored this book while in London and made arrangements to print 100,000 flyers of Jesus' tomb in India and distribute them among the British with the help of other missionaries who were sent to London for training.

When World War II broke out and the Germans launched bombing raids over England, Shams announced that God would protect His house and anyone who enters it. As a result, approximately twenty families moved into the Ahmadiyya mission house next to Fazl Mosque. Although many buildings surrounding the vicinity of the Mosque had been destroyed, Fazl Mosque was left unharmed. Two bombs fell into the Mosque's courtyard, but they failed to detonate, and were later disarmed by the British military authorities.

In 1946, after ten years of separation from his wife and two children—a sacrifice he willingly accepted for the spread of Islam Ahmadiyyat in Europe—Maulana Shams was called back to the Ahmadiyya Headquarters in Qadian to serve in various capacities.

During the Partition of the Indian subcontinent in 1947, he was appointed the Ameer of the last Ahmadi caravan departing from Qadian to Pakistan. Upon reaching the outskirts of Qadian, he halted the caravan, looked back at Qadian, and recited the same words that the Hoy Prophet[saw] recited as he departed from Mecca's city limits. Maulana Shams also proposed the name *Rabwah* for the Ahmadiyya Community's new Headquarters in Pakistan, which was approved by Hazrat Khalifatul-Masih II[ra]. He was one of only three recipients given the prestigious Khalid-e-Ahmadiyyat title, reminiscent of the great Muslim general Hazrat Khalid bin Waleed[ra], the 'Sword of Allah', whose unsurpassable skills in warfare would not allow him to achieve martyrdom despite hundreds of duels he engaged in during the battles he led against the Apostates, Romans, and Persians. In addition, the Second Khalifah[ra] indicated that one of the peripheral interpretations of the Holy Prophet's prophecy that in the Latter Days the Sun would rise from the West was fulfilled in the person of Shams (*shams* meaning *sun* in Arabic), when he returned from the West to the East.

Maulana Shams served as Nazir Islaho-Irshad (in charge of missionary work in Pakistan) until his death on 13th October 1966. He held various positions until that time including: Secretary of Bahishti Maqbarah, Managing Director of Al-Shirkat-ul-Islamiyyah, Secretary Majlis Iftaa, and President of Majlis Kaar Pardaaz. At the time of his death, he was survived by his wife and seven children.

He had written approximately seventy books in Urdu, Arabic, and English.

FOREWORD TO THE FIRST EDITION

Maulvi Shams has done me the honour of asking me to write a foreword to his interesting and enlightening treatise, which I do with pleasure.

Religion, if it is to have its natural and proper place in the spiritual life, must be founded upon fact, and the search for and the assimilation of fact is one of the aims of Islam. Maulvi Shams has certainly been assiduous in his search and he has set out the result with a skill calculated to arouse envy in a highly-placed lawyer. The results are tabulated definitely and clearly, although his lucid presentation may not be acceptable to those who would define faith as 'subscription to something which cannot be proven'. He has cleared the ground of many false assumptions, indeed, he has ruthlessly excised them, but without ridicule. It is sometimes claimed for Christianity that it has reached a final position, but how can such claim be justified when the doctrines or so-called facts upon which the religion is founded are proved to be unstable? Jesus was a prophet sent by God to declare the Truth unto the lost sheep of the House of Israel. That truth is today held to be contained in a framework of creeds and doctrines preached as Christianity in every quarter of the habitable globe, all of which deviate from the teachings of Jesus. How much, or rather, how little, does modern Christianity represent the teachings enunciated by Jesus? If, then, Christianity has deviated so far from its foundation, what basis is there for the claim that it has reached finality?

Although this volume is not large in size, it is great in achievement, and all the chapters are equal in importance and interest, although many readers claim the greatest attraction to be in the section devoted to the Resurrection and Ascension, particularly the latter. Maulvi Shams has undoubtedly thrown much light upon this debatable topic, and the new evidence he has produced reaches beyond the circumstantial. This new evidence should be well examined and considered, not judged hastily, but without prejudice and, what is equally important, without yielding to emotion through prejudiced ideas. The weakness of the orthodox position, particularly with regard to the Ascension, is manifested by the manner in which Christian apologists shrink from the discussion of so important a question. 'The question', says W. Carew Hazlitt, is 'was there a single person of credit who actually beheld the Ascension and communicated the particulars to those who have transmitted them, such as they are, to us?' The inquiry generally is shirked, not only by Christian apologists, but by critics generally, such as Viscount Amberely and W. R. Cassels. Dr. Mozley, without any attempt at proof, claims that the Ascension 'is as certain as anything in history'; while Dr. R. J. Campbell, also without production of proof, claims that 'the whole story is literally and exactly true'. Yet neither offers corroborative evidence of either the Resurrection or Ascension. What people in modern times want to know, writes F. C. Conybeare, is whether the Ascension did really happen. That is the plain issue which Bishop Gore and others both apologists and critics, seem to shirk, but which has been answered fully and clearly by Maulvi Shams.

It has also been answered by many in the seclusion of the study and library. But, to quote again F. C. Conybeare: 'Would it not be simpler in the end to tell people plainly that a legend is only a legend. They are not infants in arms. Why is it accounted so terrible for a clergyman or minister of religion to express openly in the pulpit opinions he can hear in many academical lecture rooms and often entertain in the privacy of his study?'

DUDLEY WRIGHT,
(Phil. D, P.S.P.)

FOREWORD TO THE PRESENT EDITION

God's Word revealed to the Holy Prophet Muhammad[saw]—the Holy Quran—proclaims that Jesus[as] did not die on the cross. In corroboration of this Quranic revelation, the Promised Messiah[as], Hazrat [His Holiness] Mirza Ghulam Ahmad, proposed the revolutionary theory that Jesus[as] died in India. This theory challenges the very foundation of Judeo-Christian views surrounding the advent of the Messiah. Simply put, if Jesus[as] did not die on the cross, he could not be the false prophet that Jews allege him to be citing the criteria in Deuteronomy 18:20–22 and 21:22–23, nor could he be carrying the curse of all mankind's sins as alluded to in Paul's Epistle to the Galatians 3:13. This forces Judaism to reconsider him as the fulfilment of their anticipated Messiah, and questions the Christian concept of salvation.

In *Where did Jesus Die?*, Maulana Shams[ra] illustrates that the most rational and credible explanation of Jesus' crucifixion and post-crucifixion events is the one provided by the Holy Prophet[saw] and the Promised Messiah[as]. Their account requires neither fabricated miracle nor myth. It just so happens that this is the only account that glorifies Jesus Christ[as] by exonerating him from the accursed death on the cross and restoring him the honour of a truthful prophet when judged against the criteria in the Old Testament.

This is the twelfth edition of *Where did Jesus Die?* We have supplemented this edition with new evidence from the Nag Hammadi Library discovered in 1945. This library consists of over 50 texts, many of which were believed to have been destroyed prior to this extraordinary discovery. Interestingly, several of these texts—buried for approximately 1500 years—support the Islamic perspective presented in *Where did Jesus Die?* We have documented this additional evidence in the Appendix to the Twelfth Edition.

As a further enhancement, we have reformatted the content and footnotes to facilitate readability, and verified all biblical references against the King James Version. Some references were added where they previously did not exist.

I would like to express my sincere gratitude to Naser-ud-Din Shams, Syed Sajid Ahmad, Hassan Faiyaz Khan, Syed Faraz Hussain, and Abdul Wahab Mirza for their respective contributions in validating references, reviewing the text, and formatting its content. May Almighty Allah bless them and their families for their efforts in making this publication a success.

May our Gracious Lord continue to reveal reliable facts that will exonerate His Holiness Jesus[as] from the accursed death on the cross, and enlighten this book's readers to the glorification of the Messiah[as] and the truth of Islam. *Aameen.*

Munir-ud-Din Shams
Additional Wakilut-Tasneef
London, January 2017

INTRODUCTION

The subject I am going to discuss in this book is one of great importance as it is closely associated with the beliefs of three great religions, Judaism, Christianity, and Islam.

The Jews believe that by nailing Jesus to the Cross and putting him to what was universally accepted by them as an 'accursed' death, they proved beyond any shadow of a doubt that he was a false prophet.

The Christians agree with the Jews in so far that Jesus indeed did die an 'accursed' death, but assert that this was in order to save mankind. St. Paul says in Galatians 3.13: 'Christ hath redeemed us from the curse of the law, being made a curse for us; for it is written, Cursed is everyone that hangeth on a tree.'

The reference is to Deuteronomy 21.23: 'He that is hanged is accursed of God.' They also hold that the death of Jesus on the cross, followed by his resurrection, is an essential basis of Christianity. St. Paul says in his first Epistle to the Corinthians (15:14): 'And if Christ be not risen, then is our preaching vain and your faith is also vain.' Contrary to this prevalent belief, God declared in the

Holy Quran that Jesus was one of His messengers, sent to the Lost Sheep of the House of Israel whom God out of His mercy, saved from the accursed death designed by his opponents; and caused him to die a natural death like other divine prophets.

If, therefore, we can prove, that Jesus did not die on the cross, but was taken down in a state of unconsciousness, that he lived afterward to complete his mission eventually to die a natural death, we prove also that both the Jews and the Christians are mistaken in an essential part of their beliefs. It is no exaggeration to say that present-day Christianity, founded on the 'accursed' death of Jesus, will surely crumble down at once.

In taking the Gospels as evidence of the truth of our contention that Jesus did not die on the cross, we must bear in mind the following points:

1. The Councils of Nicea and Laodicea, writes Thomas Paine[1], were held about 350 years after the time that Christ is said to have lived; and the books that now compose the New Testament were then voted by 'yeas' and 'nays' as we now vote for a law. A great many that were offered had a majority of 'nays' and were rejected. This is the way in which the New Testament came into being: 'Be this as it may, they decided by vote which of the books out of the collection they had made should be considered as the Word of God, and which should not. They rejected several; they voted others to be doubtful such as the books called the Apocrypha; and those books which had a majority of votes were voted to be the Word of

---

1. *The Age of Reason.*

God. Had they voted otherwise, all the people, since calling themselves Christians, would have believed otherwise, for the belief of the one comes from the vote of the other'.

2. They are not, therefore, the Word of God, nor did the Evangelists put forward any claim to that effect.

3. They were written very many years after the crucifixion, 'When it must have been very difficult for the writers to make an accurate record, to collect reliable and trustworthy data from the welter of hazy impressions formed in their minds during the rapid succession of events which culminated in the climax of Calvary'.

4. Numerous inconsistencies and contradictions existing in the four accounts are positive proof of their contents being doubtful and liable to be correct or incorrect.

5. Modern research has shown that the author of the fourth Gospel was not John the disciple of Jesus, and verse 24 of the last chapter of that Gospel also reveals this fact.
   Likewise, the original Hebrew text of the Matthew Gospel was lost and the author of the existing translation was an unknown person. The other two (Mark and Luke) were not the Apostles of Jesus.

6. It cannot be doubted that a historical work is often greatly affected by the personal beliefs and mentality of the historian. The various historical data mentioned in the four Gospels,

such as the generation, crucifixion and resurrection must be examined in the same manner as we examine other historical works. Like proofs must be demanded. When investigating past events we must carefully sift the evidence so as to separate the reliable from the unreliable, and accept what seems reasonable and acceptable to human intelligence in the light of other similar cases.

7. Finally, in examining the particular case of the crucifixion and resurrection of Jesus, we must bear in mind that the Gospels were written when the death of Jesus on the cross, for some reason or other, was already believed in by the majority, though not by all sects calling themselves Christians. If, therefore we find events mentioned in the Gospels which do not bear out this belief, it is because such events were so well known that they could not be easily omitted from a record of the events.

In view of the importance of the subject, I earnestly request the reader to consider the contents of this booklet carefully and without prejudice, so that he may reach the right conclusion.

Now when this book is going to the press for the sixth print, I should like to add the following to the aforesaid introduction:

In August 1939, just before World War II broke out, I printed a leaflet, a hundred thousand in number, under the caption 'The Tomb of Jesus Christ in India'. Hardly 4,000 of them were distributed in Greater London and its suburbs, when, in view of the changed circumstances I purposely postponed the distribution till the end of the War. When the war was over and the civilized world again had a chance of breathing freely, six Muslim missionaries from Qadian, India, made their appearance in London. Naturally they put up with me at the Fazl Mosque, 63, Melrose Road, London, S.W.18. I drew up a plan with the help of these missionaries for the distribution of the said leaflet. Copies were also sent by post to various other countries of Europe and America. Besides the distribution of the leaflet I was able to publish the book entitled *Where did Jesus Die?* The leaflet and the book caused a stir in London especially amongst the ecclesiastical authorities who took a serious note of the new book and the leaflet. Many of the London papers published long notes on the subject. *Wimbledon Borough News* published a 300-word article about the discovery of the Tomb of Jesus. In this article the editor writes:

> Imam Shams also sets out the facts briefly in a leaflet a hundred thousand of which are being distributed over a wide area, including Wimbledon. (*Wimbledon Borough News* 22nd February, 1946).

This article provoked comments from readers. The Editor published the correspondence following this article in the issues of 1st, 8th and 29th March, 1946 under the captions 'Why not open the tomb', 'Lessons of the cross', 'Where did Jesus Die?' and 'Tomb of Jesus' etc.

A correspondent, Mr. M. J., said:

> The belief that Jesus Christ did not die on the cross, expressed by Imam Shams, a Moslem, in your paper last week, is one which is shared even by some Christians.

J. D. Turner wrote:

> If in fact there was no death and no resurrection, as narrated in the New Testament, it seems to me that the whole foundation of organised Christianity is swept away, and where then does the Church stand? (Issue dated 13th March, 1946)

And my answer to the question 'Why not open the tomb?' was that as the tomb was believed by the inhabitants of Kashmir to be the tomb of a prophet they will never allow it to be opened until there is a strong demand and pressure by the 'Christian World'. I, however, have discussed the subject in detail in my book *Where did Jesus Die?* and have proved by authentic historical proofs, that the tomb in question is none other than the Tomb of Jesus, the prophet.

The Rev. J. Stafford Wright, M.A., Senior Tutor, Oak Hill College, in an article under the caption 'The Moslem Invasion of England' published in the weekly journal, the *Life of Faith* (London) dated 15th May, 1946 wrote about the leaflet and the book:

> A few weeks ago a student was handed a tract by an Indian. It was not a Christian tract, but a Moslem. Photographs had already appeared in the London papers of a group of Moslem missionaries who had come to convert the English. Here was proof of their activities. Since then, plenty more of these tracts have been distributed.
>
> This tract was a claim that the Promised Messiah had

come in the person of Hazrat Ahmad (1835–1908). It also bore a photograph of what was called 'The tomb of Jesus' in the town of Srinagar in Kashmir. A brief message spoke of proof that Jesus did not die on the cross, but travelled to India and died there.

A letter to the London Mosque produced a more elaborate book entitled 'Where did Jesus Die?' This book has 128 pages, and is written and published by the Imam of the London Mosque, Maulvi J. D. Shams. This branch of Islam which is responsible for propaganda is the Ahmadiyya Movement, about which an article appeared in the *Life of Faith* some months ago, from the pen of the Rev. A. R. Pittway, a missionary in Kenya who had met one of its propagandists there. It is a strongly missionary movement, and although it is regarded by some Muslims as unorthodox, it is sufficiently close to traditional Muhammadanism to be counted as fully representative of the Muhammadan faith.

The book is a carefully documented attack upon Christianity and at the end it expands the idea that Jesus went to India and died there. There are, of course, three key points of Christianity to be attacked—the death of Christ, the resurrection, and the ascension—all of which must be proved to be false. For the theory is that Jesus only fainted on the Cross, revived in the tomb, came out and met His disciples, and then tramped away to India, where ultimately He died. It is to our everlasting shame as Christians that our country should now be experiencing a Moslem invasion of this kind. But, British toleration being what it is, it is quite possible that some of this propaganda will spread. If so, it is as well to be forearmed against it.

The *Psychic News* (London) 20th April, 1946 published a photograph of the tomb of Jesus in Srinagar (Kashmir) with the description 'Here in Khanyar Street, Srinagar, Kashmir is the tomb which is believed by the Muslims to be that of Jesus. They invite investigation.'

The journal also published a statement on the Ahmadiyya evidence regarding the death of Jesus. He began his articles with the words:

> We publish this picture and its interpretation believing it will interest many spiritualists who may not be aware of the claim made that Jesus did not die at Calvary, as preached by Churches for 2,000 years. It is also a matter of historical interest in which we take no sides. Readers can consider the following statement for themselves;

After giving a short summary of the arguments from my book *Where did Jesus Die?* the paper closed its article with the words;
'Here is a chance for archaeologists.'

In the *Psychic News* of 11th May, 1946, the Editor writes:

> Our recent production of the alleged tomb of Jesus at Srinagar, Kashmir, has brought quite a number of letters from correspondence, some accepting the statement of the Muslim sect, some opposing them. Here is a selection.

Below I give the opinion of two of them:

Mr. George Rulf, of Heaton, Newcastle-on-Tyne, in a long letter says:

> I was much interested in your article about the claim of a Muslim sect that the Master, Jesus, did not die on the cross, but travelled via Persia and Afghanistan to Kashmir and eventually died at Srinagar where his body was buried.
>
> This practically tallies with a trance address, given many years ago by a well-known spirit guide. But, I think, the time has come when people should wean themselves from accepting as truth the theological fairy tales that have no foundation in fact.
>
> That guide said that he hoped we would never ask him that question, but as we had—and as he had promised us to always tell the TRUTH—he would tell us the true story, although he was afraid that it would be unpalatable to most people with orthodox leanings.
>
> He began by saying that the name Jesus was in those days as common as our name Smith.
>
> My own comment is: The Master Jesus was not known in his own day by the name of Jesus, but by his proper name of Joshua. Only much later, when the Gospel accounts were compiled, did the compilers decide to change the name to the Greek YAYZOUS (our writing: Jesus) as there had already been a Prophet Joshua and, they thought if they called the Master 'Joshua II' it might cause confusion. In this, I think, they were justified.
>
> The Guide said that the passion story was a

composition concerning the trial and death of four different persons, an insurgent general, a robber, somebody else, (I am quoting from memory as my notes are stored away) and travelling Teacher.

It happened that all had the name Joshua. This resulted in a confusion by the later chroniclers and mixed up the trials and death of these persons and made one story out of it. Actually the Master Jesus lived to a ripe old age and travelled to other lands. But, said the Guide, this did not detract anything from the greatness of a very lovable master whom he eulogised with a considerable amount of affection and respect.

My own concluding remarks are that the 'Saviour of the Cross' story is pure fabrication by ecclesiastical writers of the 5th to 6th and 7th centuries; and the people of those days were quite indignant when they were asked to wear crucifixes with the body of the master on them and strongly repudiated this idea.

But the clergy insisted, as the whole make up, i.e., creating fear, pity, and awe, suited their purpose. The world has thus been saddled with orthodoxy's high spot of gloom called 'Good Friday', and the story of a Saviour, who—through his death—is supposed to have taken on his shoulders the sins of all believing Christians, all others, of course not being 'saved', would slip straight down to Hell.

Mrs. N. E. Clark, Heathcroft, N.W.11 said:

> With reference to the article on the tomb of Jesus, Murray's 'Handbook of India, Burmah and Ceylon' refers to inscription: 'I.S.A. (Jesus)' in a mosque at Fatehpur.
> All inscriptions may be found in the 'Miftaah-ul-Tawarikh', by John Ellis, printed at Agra. In the book, 'Hafed—Prince of Persia', it is stated that Jesus travelled to India.

Free Thinkers

Below I give some extracts from an article published in the well-known London newspaper *Free Thinkers* of Sunday, 2nd June, 1946 under the heading *Christian Evidence on Ice:*

> The main theme is the Presidential Address of the Bishop of London at the annual meeting of the Christian Evidence Society held at Caxton Hall.
> The audience was about fifty people, mostly advanced in years, the proportion of women being as one to five. This constitutes a clear proof of the fact that Christian faith is fast losing its hold and the men are first to set aside its yoke.
> We have been in the habit of thinking we are in possession of the field. We are now having to realise that we are not the only people who are trying to propagate a

religious faith. We have not merely attacks on religious faith as such. We have a rival religion.

This sounded ominous, were the forces of Islam preparing to invade our sanctuaries? Would there be a formidable boosting of Buddhism? No, all this solemn warning was provoked by the fact that the Bishop had seen Orientals distributing at a tube station a booklet displaying a picture of an Indian temple, beneath which, it was alleged was the body of Jesus Christ. The Bishop quaintly added: 'The assumption that if the tomb was opened the remains would be found not entirely scientific.' This he said was another religion undertaking an intensive form of propaganda.

Since attending the meeting I have obtained the pamphlet (book) referred to. It is entitled *Where did Jesus Die?* The author is J. D. Shams and it emanates from the Mosque at Wimbledon. It is of considerable interest to those who do not reject the historicity of Jesus. The view taken is that Jesus did not die on the cross, but left Palestine after his attempted crucifixion. This was the view taken by Thomas Henry Huxley, and was propounded in fictitious form by George Moore in 'The Brook Kerith'.

Concluding Leaflet

In May, 1946, I published the following leaflet in thousands. It was sent to the Ecclesiastical authorities by post and handed over to thousands in Greater London.

'A Challenge to the Church'
Jesus died a natural death; his tomb found in India

A leaflet, one hundred thousand in number has recently been distributed in Greater London. The gist of the leaflet was that Jesus did not die on the cross, but escaped death and went to India and there died a natural death. His tomb in India has been discovered by Prophet Ahmad of Qadian, Punjab, India, in whose person the prophecy concerning the second advent of Jesus is fulfilled.

Some newspapers have published a considerable account of it, followed by a lively correspondence, whilst another has produced the photograph of the tomb as well. Moreover, I have received a pile of letters, the senders of which have shown great interest and asked for further information. To these people my book, *Where did Jesus Die?* has been sent. In this book, I have discussed this question in detail and have proved in a manner which will certainly convince the unbiased reader, that Jesus did not die on the cross, but died a natural death like other prophets of God.

Many of the readers have thought it credible and have asked for further information. One wrote: 'This statement seems to be quite feasible.'

Another writes: 'As an unorthodox Christian and seeker of truth your suggestion appeals to me since it backs up a personal belief', etc.

Many of those who have read my book have found it most interesting and convincing. For instance, one, asking for other booklets, writes:

> It is very convincing and I believe true. I should like to be a follower of Islam.

But some others, especially Roman Catholics, instead of seeking further information have written:

1. 'The discovery is a sham and a fraud.'
2. 'It is a vicious attack upon the Bible, the inspired word of God.'
3. 'Jesus Christ is alive.'
4. 'He lives to save.'

One Roman Catholic wrote:

> You have been grossly deceived by either a self-deluded fanatic or a charlatan, the like of which I might assure you, we have produced (our own particular brand) in this country.

Some of the clergy were so rude and outraged that they tried to snatch and tear up the leaflets from the hands of the distributors and others after accepting them, tore them up. To the latter group I would like to say that their attitude is unconstructive and cannot benefit them at all. Jesus Christ himself was abused in a worse manner by his opponents, the scribes and Pharisees.

We should not be antagonistic towards one another in the matter of religion. We Muslims believe that Jesus Christ was a prophet of God and that he, like other great prophets, suffered at the hands of opponents, who failed in their object to cause him to die an accursed death. The Resurrection, Ascension and the contention that he is living in heaven to save mankind are false notions. Muhammad (peace and blessings of God be upon him) was a true prophet of God who was given a perfect law. All the good points found in other scriptures are collectively found in Islamic teachings.

If any bishop, clergyman or other ecclesiastical authority thinks otherwise let him come forward and refute the arguments of my book, *Where did Jesus Die?*. I am always ready to prove my claim and to discuss it in public if any impartial and interested society will arrange it.

This is my challenge to the Church.

Finally, I would like to express my admiration of the average Englishman who is unbiased and examines everything in the light of reason and wisdom, and does not follow blindly. They are those who will enjoy peace and tranquillity of mind in the end.

In the end I would like to quote here the concluding words of the review of this book by Prof. Qazi M. Aslam, M.A., head of the Psychology Department, Karachi University, Karachi.

> Maulana Shams has written an important and interesting book that will prove a landmark in the history of the efforts on behalf of Islam which Ahmadis are putting forth so successfully in the West. (*The Sunrise,* 3rd August, 1946)

The hope expressed in the 'Review' is coming true by the grace of God, as everywhere our missionaries are spreading this idea in the West. The Dutch version of this book has been published by

N. Kluwer Deventer in Netherlands in 1959, and the Malayalam version in 1958.

The French translation is being prepared and in a short time will be on the market. Let us pray to God Almighty that He may redeem our Christian brethren from worshipping a man who was sent to propagate the worship of the One God.

J. D. Shams
1965

PREFACE

On its publication in 1945, the late Maulana J. D. Shams, writer of *Where did Jesus Die?*, met with such immense success that he has had six previous editions printed and also translated into several other languages. It faces resolutely the incident of the apparent death of Jesus Christ (on whom be peace) on the Cross; he demonstrates in this very readable book exactly what really happened. This book should be of real help in promoting a more rational discussion of the subject.

A scholar of vast learning, Maulana J. D. Shams had a distinguished career as a leading missionary of the Ahmadiyya Movement in Islam, and from 1936–1946 he was the Imam of the London Mosque; the book was written during his term of office in England. Because of the perpetual interest shown in this important subject, he had expressed the intention of printing this book in fairly superior quality. By the benevolence and mercy of God, this edition is an attempt to fulfil this desire to coincide with the International Conference on Deliverance of Jesus from the Cross scheduled to be held in June 1978 in London. It is a great privilege to be allowed to acknowledge that the financial burden for the present volume was borne entirely by Dr. Salah-ud-Din Shams, the eldest son of the author. This is done with sincere feelings and respect and esteem to others who also deserve our constant prayers.

An opportunity has been taken to update this edition in the form of the Appendix to the Seventh Edition.

M. D. SHAMS
Deputy Imam, the London Mosque
April, 1978

Where did Jesus Die?

بِسْمِ اللهِ الرَّحْمٰنِ الرَّحِيْمِ [1]

نَحْمَدُهُ وَنُصَلِّیْ عَلیٰ رَسُوْلِهِ الْکَرِیْمِ [2]

CHAPTER ONE—
PASSAGES FROM THE GOSPELS

Jesus' Prayer

When Jesus announced his claim to be the Messiah, he took all precautions for his personal safety. At one time he charged his disciples that they should tell no man that he was Jesus the Christ.[3] At another time when his opponents took counsel together to put him to death, he gave up walking openly among the Jews and went to a country near to the wilderness.[4] He even hid himself from

---

1. In the name of Allah, the Gracious, the Merciful. [Publisher]
2. We praise Him, and invoke blessings on His Noble Messenger[saw]. [Publisher]
3. Matthew 16:20
4. John 11:53, 54

them.[1] When he knew the determination of his opponents to stop his activities by force, even by killing him if they possibly could do so, Jesus went with his disciples to a hiding place known to them.[2] Then he learnt by divine revelation or from the tottering loyalty of Judas and his absence at the time, that he would be betrayed by him and that his arrest was imminent. He could see no way of escape then, except to pray with great humility, placing his forehead at the threshold of Almighty God who alone could frustrate the plans of his enemies by saving him from the clutches of death.

It appears from the accounts given in Matthew 26, Mark 14 and Luke 22 that Jesus went to Gethsemane with some of his disciples and directed them to pray, but instead they fell asleep and twice he awakened them without success.

He himself prayed with great humility saying:

> Abba, Father, all things *are* possible unto thee; take away this cup from me: nevertheless, not what I will but what thou wilt.[3]

In this manner he passed the greater part of the night in earnest prayer. On the appearance of an angel from heaven, a sign of acceptance of his prayer, he prayed more passionately.

His sweat dropped on the ground like great drops of blood.[4]

---

1. John 12:36
2. John 18:1, 2
3. Mark 14:36
4. Luke 22:44

The gist of this prayer of Jesus was that he might be saved from death, not because he was afraid of laying down his life in the way of God, but in order that the will of God about His messenger might be fulfilled against the will of his enemies. This is the meaning, as I understand, of Jesus' saying: 'Not what I will but what thou wilt.'

Had Jesus known that his death on the cross was Gods' will he would never have prayed: 'All things *are* possible unto thee, take away this cup from me'; i.e., the cup of death which his opponents had held up to his lips for him to drink.

The Cup was Taken Away

We believe the aforementioned prayer of Jesus was heard by God and accepted. Our belief is based on the following grounds:

1. Jesus himself claims that God heard his prayers:

   Father, I thank thee that thou hast heard me. And I knew that thou hearest me always.[5]

He also enjoins others to pray and says that God will answer their prayers.[6] He says also:

   What man is there of you, whom if his son ask bread, will

---

5. John 11:41–42
6. Mark 11:24

he give him a stone? Or if he ask a fish, will he give him a serpent?[1]

Now, if even Jesus' own prayer, uttered in agony with such earnestness and sincerity, and concerning so important a matter as his threatened death by crucifixion was disregarded, his injunctions to his disciples that they should pray for what they required and his statement that their prayers will be answered would seem to have little meaning. We have no option, therefore, but to believe that God did hear his prayer and thus saved him from the 'accursed' death.

2. Concerning the acceptance of his prayer, the following texts from the Psalms may be quoted:

> For dogs have compassed me: the assembly of the wicked have inclosed me: they pierced my hands and my feet...But be not thou far from me, O Lord: O my strength, haste thee to help me...For he hath not despised nor abhorred the affliction of the afflicted, neither hath he hid his face from him; but when he cried unto him, he heard.[2]

Also in Psalm 34 we read:

> Many are the afflictions of the righteous, but the Lord

---

1. Matthew 7:9–10
2. Psalms 22:16–24

delivereth him out of them all. He keepeth all his bones: not one of them is broken.[1]

In John 19:23 to 36, both the Psalms have been applied to Jesus Christ. In regard to the second it will be remembered that whilst the limbs of the two thieves put on the cross with Christ were broken, Jesus was left untouched. Thus, God, hearing his prayer, saved him from the 'accursed' death.

3. Jesus himself believed that God had accepted his prayer and that he would not die on the cross, wherefore when he realised his terrible condition, nailed on to the cross without seemingly the slightest chance of escape, for the first time a doubt assailed him which found expression in the despairing cry, 'My God, my God, why hast thou forsaken me?'[2] God did not forsake him. He had prepared his deliverance. If, however, we assume that he died on the cross, then we must think that God did, indeed, forsake him, a consequence totally at variance with his words: 'Behold, the hour cometh, yea, is now come, that ye shall be scattered, every man to his own, and shall leave me alone: and yet I am not alone, because the Father is with me.'[3]

4. All scriptures are unanimous that God hears the prayers of the righteous but not of the wicked, nor of His enemies. See, for

---

1. Psalms 34:19–20
2. Matthew 27:46
3. John 16:32

example, Psalms 18:6 and 66: 18–20; Jeremiah 29:13, and Job 22: 27. We also read in John:

> We know that God heareth not sinners: but if any man be a worshipper of God, and doeth his will, him he heareth.[1]

If then we deny that God heard and answered the prayer of Jesus, we have no alternative but to believe that Jesus was a sinner, and not a righteous person who did according to the will of God. And to believe this about a person like Jesus, who was a prophet of God, is certain blasphemy. We read in Hebrews about this prayer of Jesus:

> Who in the days of his flesh, when he had offered up prayers and supplications with strong crying and tears unto him that was able to save him from death, and was heard in that he feared.[2]

Thus, the Jews failed in their plan and God saved Jesus, a righteous and God-fearing person, from an 'accursed' death.

---

1. John 9:31
2. Hebrews 5:7

Was Jesus the Cursed One?

Jesus said to his opponents:

> Woe unto you, scribes and Pharisees, hypocrites! for ye shut up the kingdom of heaven against men: for ye neither go in *yourselves*, neither suffer ye them that are entering to go in.[1]

Again he says: 'He that believeth not shall be damned.'[2] Now the Pharisees believed that they caused Jesus to die an 'accursed' death and if this was true—and St. Paul testifies to it—then according to their law they proved conclusively that Jesus was a false prophet and that they were right in rejecting him and, therefore, will not be damned for it.

In view of the real meaning of the word 'cursed', a cursed man cannot be a prophet and beloved of God, for a man cannot be a cursed one unless his relationship with God is cut and his heart becomes empty of His love and knowledge; unless he is deprived too, of the mercy and grace of God. He must be in error like Satan and at enmity with God; thus, Satan is named the 'Accursed One'.

Of a righteous and holy person like Christ, who claimed to be the light of the world—the beloved of God that God heard his prayers—can we believe that he was cursed of God and had no relationship with Him, and that his heart was overcome by error and disbelief? Bearing in mind these facts, we must necessarily

---

1. Matthew 23:13
2. Mark 16:16

reject the possibility of Jesus' death on the cross which would have made him as one accursed.

Rising of the Saints

The third argument, to prove that Jesus did not die on the cross, is contained in Matthew, chapter 27:

> And the graves were opened; and many bodies of the saints which slept arose, and came out of the graves after his resurrection, and went into the holy city, and appeared unto many.[1]

It is obvious that this occurrence cannot be taken in its literal sense because if it were literally true, we would not fail to find reference to such an extraordinary, unprecedented, and supernatural event, but there is none to be found; and Matthew is the only Gospel writer to mention it, while the remaining three have not bothered even to hint at it. Had it been true, it would have been an excellent opportunity for the Jews to question these resurrected holy men as to the truth of Christ, and if they had vouched for him, the Jews would have accepted him without further question. Let me quote Thomas Paine on this story:

> It is an easy thing to tell a lie, but it is difficult to support the lie after it is told. The writer of the book of Matthew

---

1. Matthew 27:52–53

should have told us who the saints were that came to life again and went into the city, and what became of them afterwards, and who it was that saw them—for he is not hardy enough to say that he saw them himself—whether they came out naked, and all in natural buff, he-saints and she-saints; or whether they came fully dressed, and from where they got their clothes; whether they went to their former habitations and reclaimed their wives, their husbands, and their property, and how they were received; whether they entered ejectments for the recovery of their possessions or brought actions of criminal conspiracy against the rival interlopers; or whether they died again, or went back to their graves alive and buried themselves. Strange indeed that an army of saints should return to life and nobody knows who they were, or who it was who saw them and that not a word more should be said upon the subject, nor have these saints anything to tell us! Had it been the prophets who (as we are told) had formerly prophesied of these things, they must have had a great deal to say. They could have told us everything, and we should have had posthumous prophecies, with notes and commentaries upon the first, a little better at least than we have now. Had it been Moses, and Aaron, and Joshua, and Samuel, and David, not an unconverted Jew would have remained in Jerusalem. Had it been John the Baptist, and the saints of the times then present, everybody would have known them, and they would have out-preached and out-framed all the other apostles. But instead of this, these saints are made to pop up like Jonah's gourd in the night, for no purpose at all but to wither in the morning.[1]

No doubt if we take Matthew literally, we have to face all these questions, but the truth is that this verse, as Ahmad the Promised Messiah writes, refers to a vision seen by certain righteous men, and it is well-known that such visions are capable of interpretation, as Joseph interpreted the dream of Pharaoh.

It is most interesting that in an Arabic book *Ta'tir-ul-Anam* (page 289), on the interpretation of dreams and written over 600 years ago by a leading authority on the subject, Shaikh Abdul-Ghani Nablusi, we read:

> If anyone sees in a dream that the dead have come out of their graves and have made for their homes, the interpretation of this is: that a great man who is in prison would be released from the prison and would be rescued.

Now as this vision was seen at the time of the resurrection, the inference is obvious that his death was only apparent and that in consequence of the swoon which led his persecutors to believe that he was dead his release from the sepulchre in which he had been lodged was effected. In short, this vision seen by certain God-fearing persons revealed to them that Jesus was not dead but was like a prisoner in the tomb from whence he escaped to a place of safety.

---

1. *The Age of Reason* by Thomas Paine

Sign of Jonah the Prophet

Jesus when called upon by the Jews to show them a sign said:

> An evil and adulterous generation seeketh after a sign; and there shall no sign be given to it, but the sign of the prophet Jonas: for as Jonas was three days and three nights in the whale's belly; so shall the Son of Man be three days and three nights in the heart of the earth.[1]

This saying of Jesus settles the question once and for all. The Jews sought to kill him, but he escaped death. They did all that lay in their power to put him to death but God delivered him from their hands. Thus, his escape was a sign for the Jews. The words of Jesus indicated the way in which the sign was to be shown and the manner in which he was to be delivered from the hands of his murderous foes. He was to be placed in the belly of the earth like one dead, but his case was to be like that of Jonah in the belly of the whale. The latter, while in the belly of the whale, was not dead but alive. Similarly, Jesus was to be alive, not dead in the bosom of the earth. Jesus, by comparing his case to that of Jonah, clearly indicated the way in which he was to escape. He was to enter the sepulchre alive and come out of it alive, just as Jonah had entered his living sepulchre alive and had come out of it alive. The prophecy of Jesus strikes a death blow to the notion that he died an 'accursed' death on the cross.

---

1. Matthew 12:39–40

The Dream of Pilate's Wife

> When he [Pilate] was set down on the judgment seat, his wife sent unto him, saying, Have thou nothing to do with that just man: for I have suffered many things this day in a dream because of him.[1]

This warning, given to Pilate by God through his wife, at the very commencement of the trial, was a clear revelation of the will of God to Pilate who himself believed in Jesus' innocence, and knew that for envy the Jews had delivered him up.[2] What was then the purpose of this dream which God showed to the Governor's wife, if he did not intend to save Jesus from death? When Herod sought to kill Jesus in his childhood, Joseph also was warned against Herod's evil intention, by way of a dream in order to save Jesus' life and, accordingly, Joseph took him and his mother to Egypt.[3] Likewise, God revealed His will to Pilate through his wife. Pilate did deliver Jesus to his enemies when they threatened to complain against him to Caesar, were he to release Jesus.[4] Nevertheless, he secretly did everything possible to save Jesus from death. He prolonged the trial until a very late hour on Friday, knowing it was unlawful for Jews to keep anybody on the cross after nightfall on the Sabbath day. The time left for crucifixion would be so short

---

1. Matthew 27:19
2. Matthew 27:18
3. Matthew 2:13
4. John 19:12

that it would be impossible for Jesus to die on the cross. It was three hours only, not at all enough to cause death.

The centurion appointed to execute the order of crucifixion showed great sympathy towards Jesus and, according to Luke, believed in his righteousness. Likewise, the soldiers who broke the legs of the two thieves put on the cross with Jesus did not break Jesus' legs. Moreover, a person, who had apparently no connection whatever with Jesus, hurriedly appeared on the scene. He was a rich man named Joseph of Arimathea, a secret disciple who remained secret for fear of Jews, as John's Gospel describes him. This Joseph of Arimathea besought Pilate that he might take away the body of Jesus. And, contrary to prevailing custom, Pilate allowed him to do so, without making the least query about this new person. Then he and a physician named Nicodemus took the body in their care, all according to plan. They did not bury him with others in a common burial ground but laid him with great care in a new tomb, which Joseph had hewn out of the rock in his own garden. There they could treat him without being noticed by the Jews now busy with their religious ceremonies of the Sabbath day, the Sabbath being a high day. Jesus, after he had recovered, came out of the sepulchre. Thus we see that Pilate successfully carried out his plans to rescue Jesus from death, and fulfilled the purpose of God for which He had shown the aforesaid vision to his wife.

CHAPTER TWO— THE JUDGMENT

Circumstantial Evidence[a]

Once a great controversy took place between a number of Muslims on one side and a number of Christians on the other, concerning the 'accursed' death of Jesus on the cross and his resurrection. The Muslims took an 'accursed' death as a great insult to Jesus, one of the great messengers of God, but the Christians took it as a divine gift for humanity. It so happened that the Christians lodged a petition in the court against the Muslims, and the case was heard by two independent judges of high understanding. After the hearing, they issued the following judgment.

(a) I have written up the 'Circumstantial Evidence' in the form of a judgment. It may be easier thus for my readers to understand.

A Christian (C) versus a Muslim (M).
Re Jesus's Death on the Cross and his Resurrection.

This is a suit regarding an important historical event. The plaintiff C brought this suit on 8th April, against M who denied the accursed death of Jesus. On the pleadings of the parties, the following issues were determined for trial.

1. Did Jesus die on the cross?
2. Did he rise from the dead?
3. Did he rise with an astral body or with a body made of flesh and bones?

The trial lasted two days, during which the parties concerned argued their views. Having heard both sides and having examined the 'pros' and 'cons' we hereby give our judgment impartially. The evidence of C on whom the proof of the issues was laid, consists of four written documents, about which C has claimed that they were written by eyewitnesses, viz., saints Matthew, Mark, Luke, and John, aided by the inspiration of the Omniscient God. But on examination, these documents are not proved legally. They do not bear the signatures of the witnesses, nor do they contain proof of having been written under divine inspiration. As, however, they are considered the most ancient documents on the contention, we could not ignore them altogether. Let us see how far they help us in deciding the aforesaid issues.

Issues

The three issues are so closely connected that they should be decided at one and the same time. The evidence for C on these issues is very conflicting.

The four witnesses differ among themselves not only on trivial but also important points. Here are the important points of difference:

1. *The Betrayer and his Accomplices*—Matthew and Mark say that Judas (who betrayed Jesus) with a great multitude, *from* the chief priests and elders of the people, came to Gethsemane. But Luke says that the chief priests and captains of the temple and the elders *themselves* came to arrest Jesus.[1]

2. *How Jesus was Arrested*—Matthew, Mark, and Luke say that Judas gave the multitude a sign saying, '*Whomsoever I shall kiss,* that same is he: hold him fast.' And forthwith he came to Jesus, and said, 'Hail master', and *kissed him*. And Jesus said unto him, Friend, wherefore art thou come? Then came they and laid hands on Jesus, and took him.'[2]

   But John gives quite a different account of this arrest. According to him, on the arrival of Judas with a band of men, *Jesus on his own accord went forth and said to them: 'Whom seek ye?'* They answered him: 'Jesus of Nazareth', Jesus replied: 'I am he.' And Judas also stood with them. As he said this they went

---

1. Luke 22:52.
2. Matthew 26:47–49

backward and fell to the ground. Jesus repeated his question and they reiterated their answer. Jesus said: 'I have told you that I am he. If therefore you seek me, let these go their way.' Then Peter cut off the right ear of the High Priest's servant. Then they took Jesus and bound him.[1]

3. *Timing of Peter's Attack*—Luke and John say that the ear of the High Priest's servant was cut off *before* the arrest of Jesus, but Matthew and Mark say it was cut off *after* his arrest.

4. *The End of Judas*—Matthew says that Judas repented himself and brought back the thirty pieces of silver to the chief priests and elders who refused to take them back, but he cast them down in the temple and went *and hanged himself. The chief priests and elders took counsel and bought with the sum the Potter's field* to bury strangers in. Wherefore the field was called 'the field of blood'.[2]

The other three are silent on this point, but in the Acts, which is supposed to be written by Luke, we read, Peter said that *Judas himself purchased that field with the reward of iniquity and falling headlong he burst asunder* in the midst, and all his bowels gushed out.[3]

5. *The Bearer of the Cross*—Matthew and Mark say: 'A man of Cyrene, Simon by name, him they compelled to bear his cross...

---

1. John 18:3–8, 10, 12
2. Matthew 27:3–8
3. The Acts 1:18

unto a place called Golgotha, that is to say, a place of a skull.'[1] John's account is that Jesus *himself* bearing his cross went forth into a place called the place of a skull.[2]

6. *The Sign over Jesus*—The four witnesses do not agree in quoting the very short inscription which, as they say, was set up over Jesus' head when he was put on the cross:
    Matthew: 'This is Jesus the King of the Jews' (27:37).
    Mark: 'The King of the Jews' (15:26).
    Luke: 'This is the King of the Jews' (23:38).
    John: 'Jesus of Nazareth, the King of the Jews' (19:19)

7. *The other Two Crucified Men*—Matthew and Mark say that the thieves who were put on the cross with Jesus also reviled him. But Luke says that one of them railed on him but the other rebuked him saying: 'Dost not thou fear God?' and he said to Jesus: 'Lord, remember me when thou comest into thy kingdom', and Jesus promised him that he would be with him in Paradise the very same day.[3]

    And John has not even hinted at this important conversation between the three crucified.

8. *The Time of Crucifixion.*—Mark says: 'It was the (*third hour*) when they crucified him.'[4] But John, says it was about the (*sixth*

---

1. Matthew 27:32–33
2. John 19:17
3. Luke 23:39–43
4. Mark 15:25

hour) when Pilate delivered Jesus to the Jews.[1] Matthew and Luke only mention that from the sixth hour there was darkness over all the land unto the ninth hour.

9. *How Jesus Gave up the Ghost—*
   Matthew: 'Jesus, when he had cried again with a loud voice, yielded up the ghost.'[2]
   Mark: 'And Jesus cried with a loud voice, and gave up the ghost.'[3]
   Luke: 'And when Jesus had cried with a loud voice, he said, Father, into thy hands I commend my spirit: and having said thus, he gave up the ghost.'[4]
   John: 'When Jesus therefore had received the vinegar, he said, It is finished: and he bowed his head, and gave up the ghost.'[5]

10. *When the Centurion said Jesus was Righteous and the Son of God—*
    Matthew: The centurion and they that were with him seeing the earthquake and other things feared greatly saying, 'Truly this was the Son of God.'[6]
    Mark: The centurion when he saw that Jesus so cried out

---

1. John 19:14
2. Matthew 27:50
3. Mark 15:37
4. Luke 23:46
5. John 19:30
6. Matthew 27:54

and gave up the ghost said: 'Truly this man was the Son of God.'[1]

Luke: He glorified God saying: 'Certainly this was a righteous man.'[2]

11. *Who was Joseph of Arimathea—*
    Matthew says he was Jesus' disciple (27:57).
    Mark (15:43) and Luke (23:50–51) say that he was an honourable counsellor which also waited for the Kingdom of God.
    John says he was a disciple of Jesus but secretly for fear of the Jews (19:38).

12. *Burial of the Body*—The rich man Joseph went to Pilate and begged the body of Jesus, and Pilate without making any enquiry, as Matthew and John state, and after inquiring from the centurion about Jesus' death, as Mark and Luke say, he permitted him to take the body. Then he alone wrapped it in a linen cloth and laid it in his own new tomb which he had hewn out of the rock, as Matthew, Mark, and Luke say, and he and Nicodemus both, as John states, laid him in the sepulchre.

---

1. Mark 15:39
2. Luke 23:47

Likewise, they differ concerning the events connected with Jesus' resurrection which followed the crucifixion.

1. *Who Came First to the Sepulchre, and When?*—Matthew says that as it *began to dawn* towards the first day of the week, came Mary Magdalene and *the other* Mary to see the sepulchre (28:1). Mark says: Early in the morning at the rising of the sun (16:2). Luke says: Very early in the morning (24:1).
John's account is: Early, when it was yet dark (20:1).

    Then Matthew (28:1) and Mark (16:1) say there were two Marys, and Luke (24:10) says there were Mary Magdalene and Joanna, and Mary the mother of James, and other women.

    But John's account is that Mary Magdalene came alone (20:1).

2. *The Earthquake and the Angel*—Matthew 28:2 tells us: 'And, behold, there was a great earthquake: for the angel of the Lord descended from heaven, and came and rolled back the stone from the door, and sat upon it.'

    The other three say nothing about this natural phenomenon of the earthquake, nor of the rolling back of the stone and the sitting upon it. According to their accounts no one was sitting on the stone. Mark (16:4–5) says that when the two Marys came they found the stone was already rolled away. And entering into the sepulchre they saw *a young man sitting* on the right side, and they were frightened. Luke (24:4) says there were *two men* not sitting but *standing up*. And John (20:12) says they were *two angels both sitting in the sepulchre* one at the head and the other at the feet.

3. *Who Broke the News of Jesus' Rising?*—Matthew (28:6) says: *The angel* who was sitting on the stone informed the two Marys, saying: 'He is not here; for he is risen.' Mark (16:6) says: The men sitting inside the sepulchre told them the same.

Luke (24:4–6) says: The two men standing by while the women were inside the sepulchre and were perplexed at not finding the body, told them: 'He is not here, but is risen.'

But John (20:1–15) tells a totally different story. He says: 'As Mary Magdalene saw the stone taken away from the sepulchre she ran away and came to Peter and the other disciple whom Jesus loved, and said they have taken away the Lord and we know not where they laid him. They came running to the spot and one after the other entered into the sepulchre and saw the linen cloth lying there and the napkin, that was about his head, wrapped together in a place by itself. After having seen this they went back home. But Mary stood without the sepulchre weeping, and as she wept she looked into the sepulchre and saw two angels sitting who asked her, "Woman! why weepest thou?" She had hardly finished her answer when she turned back and saw Jesus standing, whom she took first for the gardener, but knew him when he spoke to her.'

4. *The Message of Jesus and Who Delivered it?*—Matthew (28:5–10) says that the angel sitting on the stone told the two Marys: 'Go quickly and tell his disciples that he is risen from the dead, and behold, he goeth before you into Galilee, there shall ye see him. I have told you. When they were on their way Jesus also met them and gave the same message.'

Mark (16:7) says that the man sitting within the sepulchre delivered the same message.

Luke does not mention that the two men gave any message for the disciples.

John (20:17), however, says that Jesus himself asked Mary to tell his brethren: 'I ascend unto my Father and your Father; and to my God and your God.'

5. *Did They Convey the Message?*—Matthew does not say anything about it, but it appears from verse 16 of chapter 28, that they did convey the message.

But Mark says that they went quickly and fled trembling and amazed, neither said they anything to any man; for they were afraid.

Luke says that the women told the disciples that Jesus is risen and John says that Mary informed them what Jesus had told her.

6. *How did they receive the news?*—

Matthew says nothing about it.

Mark says: When they heard that he was alive and had been seen of her, they believed not.

Luke says: Their word seemed to them as idle tales and they believed them not.

John is silent upon this point.

7. *Where did Jesus meet them first?*—

Matthew says (as soon as they heard the message): The eleven disciples went away into Galilee, to a mountain which Jesus had appointed for them. And when they saw him they worshipped him, but some doubted (28:16–17). Mark says: First he appeared to Mary (16:9), then he appeared in another form unto two of them (16:12), and then he appeared unto the eleven as they sat at meat and upbraided them for their unbelief and hardness of heart, because they believed not them which had seen him after he was risen (16:14).

Luke (24:33–36) clearly contradicts Matthew, for he says that Jesus met his eleven disciples in Jerusalem during the evening of the very day he rose.

John corroborates Luke, saying that Jesus unexpectedly came to the place where his disciples were assembled 'for fear of the Jews'.[1]

From the aforesaid examples taken from the statements of the four witnesses for the plaintiff, we conclude the following:

1. These statements cannot be described as the word of God, nor can they have been inspired by God.

2. None of the four accounts seems to us to be an eyewitness account or even an account based on reliable sources. For instance, one says that at the time of Jesus' arrest the chief priests and the elders were present, the other denies it. One says that Jesus appointed a mountain in Galilee at which to meet them, and there he met them. The other says that the

---
1. John 20:19

meeting took place in Jerusalem. These accounts cannot have been written by the disciples as they knew where the meeting was to take place, because both say that the eleven disciples were present at the meeting. Likewise, some say that Judas, who betrayed Jesus, let the band know about Jesus by kissing his hand; another denies it when he says that it was Jesus himself who made himself known to them.

Consequently, their evidence is self-contradictory. Without hesitation, therefore, we declare that these accounts are not the accounts of eyewitnesses, but are based on hearsay, and do not even give the source of the information. Their statements that Jesus died on the cross and that he rose from the dead cannot be taken as genuine even if we suppose the writers to be the disciples of Jesus at the time of his arrest, for they deserted Jesus and fled. Peter, who followed him to the palace of the chief priests, is convicted by the four accounts of wilful lying three times. According to these accounts, none of Jesus' disciples were present at the time of his supposed death nor at the time when his supposed resurrection took place. We have no option, therefore, but to say that the evidence is insufficient to prove the important points on which, as the plaintiff claims, depends the salvation of the world.

Now we give below, briefly, the main points from the defendant's statement defending Jesus against the charge of an accursed death, and asserting that he was unconscious when he was taken down from the cross.[a]

---

[a] Points already discussed in the previous chapter have been left out.

CHAPTER TWO—THE JUDGMENT

1. The three hours' suspension was insufficient to cause death. Sometimes the crucified man did not die until the third day.[b]

   Pilate wondered how Jesus could have expired so soon.[2] His wonder was due to his experience that the time was not long enough to cause death. Pilate, Joseph, and the centurion—all three—were sympathisers of Jesus. They naturally wished to save him from death.

2. The two thieves who remained on the cross for the same space of time as did Jesus were both alive, and to kill them their legs were broken. Jesus was spared this ordeal.[3]

3. Blood and water flowed out immediately[4] when the soldier with a spear, pierced his right side, as the ancient pictures show; a sure sign of life and the circulation of the blood.

(b) 'The express office of the guards with their centurion was to prevent the removal of the body. This was necessary from the lingering character of the death, which sometimes did not supervene even for three days, and was at last, the result of gradual benumbing and starvation (Euseb. H.E. VIII, 8; Sen, Prov. 3), but for this guard the sufferers might have been taken down and recovered (as in the case of Sandokes: Herod VII, 194) as was actually done in the case of a friend of Josephus though only one survived out of three' (Dictionary of the Bible by Sir William Smith and Rev. J. M. Fuller, M. A. Lond. 1893, Crucifixion.)

2. Mark 15:44
3. John 19:32–33
4. John 19:34

4. After he was taken down from the cross, it was not to his enemies, but to his friends, that his body was given.[1]

5. The haste with which his friends tried to secure his body bespeak a desire on their part to save him whom apparently they had not yet given up for dead.

6. The steps taken by the Jews to have a guard posted at his sepulchre also shows that they were not sure of his death. Had they been certain of his death, it would not have mattered to them at all if his disciples had stolen his body. The reason given, 'lest his disciples come by night, and steal him away, and say unto the people, He is risen from the dead'[2] is ridiculous because they could have said if he were risen let him show himself to the people and then they could have re-arrested him. The real reason for their demand for the guard was that they were not sure of his death.

7. Pilate did not wish to have Jesus crucified, and nothing would have pleased him more than to see him delivered. And he actually gave every direct and secret aid to save Jesus. His wife's vision must have induced him to do all that was in his power to deliver Jesus from his enemies.

8. The soldiers and the centurion who refrained from ensuring the death of Jesus by the breaking of his legs, as well as the soldiers

---

[1]. John 19:38
[2]. Matthew 27:64

who pretended to have fallen asleep during their watch, must have been, like their governor, sympathisers of Jesus.

9. The tomb in which Jesus was laid, hewn out of a rock, was like a chamber in which a number of men could remain without being suffocated. It belonged to a devoted friend who must have lavished care on him so as to restore him to consciousness and health.

On Sunday, the day next to the Sabbath, the Jews were free to visit the spot. But early in the morning while it was still dark Jesus was not there. The stone had been rolled away and the body was not seen in the sepulchre. Shortly afterwards he was seen by Mary, who, at first, took him for the gardener.[1] Probably he had disguised himself in the gardener's dress, so that he might not be recognised by the Jews and re-arrested and placed upon the cross again.

10. He sent a message to his disciples to depart for the distant provinces of Galilee, saying that he would go before them and would see them there.[2] He left Jerusalem in a great hurry; for he knew the Jews would soon come to know that he had left the tomb and would start a search for him.

11. He took all precautions against being re-arrested by the Jews. He met his disciples only; not openly, but in secret, or in out of the way places. Even then he did not stay long with them,

---

1. John 20:15
2. Matthew 28:7

made no public appearance,[1] and suffered hunger and thirst. When he met his disciples, he asked them whether they could give him something to eat, and he ate in their presence.[2] To his disciples who thought him a spirit he said: 'Behold my hands and my feet, that it is I myself, handle me, and see, for a spirit hath not flesh and bones as ye see me have.'[3]

Thomas, who doubted that the other disciples had seen him, was asked to put his fingers in the prints of the nails.[4]

And the 'ointment of Jesus' or 'ointment of the Apostles' was prepared for Jesus by his disciples to heal his wounds.

All these factors clearly show that he came out of the sepulchre with his wounded physical body. Having compared this evidence with that offered by C, we find M's case the more reasonable and worthy of acceptance. As a result of our finding we declare that plaintiff C, not having produced reliable and convincing evidence has failed on the issue. Accordingly, we decide that there is no proof of Jesus' death on the cross. Consequently, he could not have risen from the dead. A reasonable person can read between the lines of the conflicting statements of the four witnesses for the plaintiff, that Jesus, when taken down from the cross, was not dead. He had swooned. Afterwards he recovered. He came out from the sepulchre with his human body of clay. Plaintiff C, has failed to answer the question that if Jesus came out with a spiritual body, where had his mortal body gone?

---

1. The Acts 10:40–41
2. Luke 24:41–43
3. Luke 24:38–39
4. John 20:27

Likewise, he could not answer the question that if Jesus had not been aided by his friends from where did he obtain the dress in which he reappeared to Mary Magdalene when she took him for the gardener? He had some clothes on. From where did this clothing come? His own garments had been taken by the soldiers, and the grave clothes were in the tomb. Moreover, the two eyewitnesses (Joseph of Arimathea and Nicodemus) who took the body and laid it in the tomb and saw what happened afterwards are not called by the plaintiff to be examined and the four written documents bear no record that the two believed that Jesus had risen from the dead.

We have no option, therefore, but to dismiss his case, which we hereby do.

(Signed) X, Y.   (Signed) A, Z.

CHAPTER THREE—
THE STORY
OF THE RESURRECTION

A Reasonable Explanation

Below, I reproduce a reasonable explanation of the story of the resurrection reported in the four Gospels, by two learned scholars who have thoroughly examined the four accounts of the Gospel writers.

1. Professor Heinrich Eberhard Gottlobe Paulus (1761–1861), who in 1789 was called to Jena as Professor of Oriental Languages, was succeeded in 1793 to the third ordinary professorship of theology. He was a member of the Bavarian Educational Council in 1807–1811. In 1811 he went to

Heidelberg as Professor of Theology and remained there until his death. He writes in *The Life of Jesus* (1828):

> The resurrection of Jesus must be brought under the same category (premature burial) if we are to hold fast to the facts that the disciples saw him in his natural body with the print of the nails in his hands and that he took food in their presence. Death from crucifixion was in fact due to a condition of rigour, which extended gradually inwards. It was slowest of all deaths. Josephus mentioned in his *Contra Apionem* that it was granted to him as a favour by Titus, at Tekoa, that he might have three crucified men, whom he knew, taken down from the cross. Two of them died but one recovered. Jesus, however, 'died' surprisingly quickly. The loud cry which he uttered, immediately before his head sank, shows that his strength was far from being exhausted, and that what supervened was only a death-like trance. In such trances the process of crying continues until corruption sets in. This alone proves that the process is complete and that death has actually taken place. In the case of Jesus, as in that of others, the vital spark would have been gradually extinguished had not Providence mysteriously effected on behalf of its favourite that which, in the cases of others was sometimes effected in more obvious ways by human skill and care. The lance thrust, which we are to think of rather as a mere surface wound served the purpose of a phlebotomy. The cool grave and the aromatic unguents continued the process of resurrection until finally the storm and the earthquake

aroused Jesus to full consciousness. Fortunately, the earthquake also had the effect of rolling away the stone from the mouth of the grave. The Lord stripped off the grave clothes and put on a gardener's dress. That was what made Mary, as we are told in John XX-15, to take him for the gardener. Through the women he sends a message to his disciples bidding them meet him in Galilee, and himself sets out to go thither. At Emmaus as the dusk was falling, he met two of his followers, who at first failed to recognise him because his countenance was so disfigured by his sufferings. But his manner of giving thanks at the breaking of the bread, and the nail prints in the uplifted hands, revealed to them who he was. From them he learns where his disciples are, returns to Jerusalem, and appears unexpectedly among them. This is the explanation of the apparent contradiction between the message pointing to Galilee and the appearance in Jerusalem.

In this way Jesus lived with them for forty days, spending part of that time with them in Galilee, in consequence of the ill-treatment which he had undergone, he was capable of continuous exertion. He lived quietly and gathered strength for the brief moments in which he appeared among his own followers and taught them. When he felt his end drawing near he returned to Jerusalem. On the Mount of Olives, in the early sunlight, he assembled his followers for the last time. He lifted up his hands to bless them and with hands still raised in benediction he moved away from them. A cloud interposes itself between them and him, so that their eyes cannot follow him. As he disappeared, there stood before them, clothed in white, the two dignified figures, who were really among the secret adherents of Jesus in Jerusalem. These men exhorted them not to stand waiting there but to be up and doing.

Where Jesus really died, they never knew, and so they came to describe his departure as an ascension.

2. Mr. Ernest Brougham Docker, District Court Judge, Sydney, has written a valuable book on this subject ('If Jesus did not Die on the Cross' 1920), in which he has scrutinised the whole evidence of the Gospels as a judge examines the evidence of a case. Below I reproduce his opinion concerning the resurrection.

The idea that dead bodies may be reanimated was prevalent in the time of our Lord, and for many hundreds of years, both before and after; in fact, wherever scientific investigation has been undeveloped. We have one instance in the history of Elijah, two in that of Elisha; there are three recorded in the gospels, besides that of Jesus himself and two in the Acts (1:18). Irenaeus speaks of frequent instances where 'the spirit has returned to the ex-animated body, and the man has been granted to the prayers of the Church'.

An interesting instance of this belief, at the present day in an unscientific people is to be found in an article by the Rev. W. Montgomery, entitled *Schweitzer as Missionary* (*Hibbert Journal*, July, 1914, p. 885):

'...The things which impress natives most is the use of anaesthetics, the girls in the mission school write letters to those in a school in Europe. In one of those letters you may read: "Since the doctor came here wonderful things are happening. First, he kills sick people; then he cures them; then he raises them to life again." What larger reputation could a wonder-worker desire?'

And the following extract (*Physical Culture and Health,* 15th July, 1912), seems to show that even skilled physicians may be mistaken in pronouncing death to have taken place in certain cases:

'Bringing the Dead to Life—A remarkable device has just been introduced by a German. It is styled the "pulmotor" and it has been successfully used on people pronounced dead by physicians, bringing them back to life, and what is more, in perfect health. A young man named Hass, asphyxiated by coal gas, whom his friends after three hours' work failed to restore to consciousness, was given up as dead (p. 17). After three hours' work with the pulmotor the man was able to sit up and express wonder and thanks declaring that he felt as well as before he was overcome. A doctor who was called in before the apparatus was employed, said that, speaking medically, Hass was in a state of death when he arrived. Hass is the fifth man who has been "called back".'

That the signs of death are sometimes simulated in the still living body and that delicate test necessary to ascertain the real fact, is manifest from the following passage from *Taylor's Medical Jurisprudence* (sixth edition, p. 243), this quotation is taken from 'The Lancet', vol. 1, 1900, under the heading *Premature Burial*:

'Cases have undoubtedly presented themselves in which persons labouring under concussion, syncope, catalepsy, hysteria, or lifelessness from exhaustion have been pronounced dead by by-standers merely because there happened to be inanimation, coldness of the surface, and no outward signs of respiration or circulation. If the decision of the question of life or death was always left to such persons and internments were to follow in a few hours upon their dictation, there is no doubt living bodies would be exposed to the risk of premature burial. But this can rarely happen in any civilized country of Europe and then only as the result of gross or culpable neglect.' (p. 18)

The Editor says (p. 246):

'...The circumstances on which we may rely as furnishing conclusive evidence are the following:

(1) The absence of circulation and respiration for at least *an hour,* the stethoscope being always employed; (2) the gradual cooling of the body, the trunk remaining warm while members are cold; and (3) as the body cools the supervention of a rigid state of the muscles successively attacking the limbs and trunk, and ultimately spreading through the whole muscular system. When these conditions are observed the proof of death is conclusive.'

Applying these principles to the instances of revivification above mentioned, if they had happened at the present day, should we have any hesitation in saying that the Shunamite lad was unconscious from sunstroke; that Eutychus was stunned by his fall; that the daughter of Jairus was suffering from exhaustion from her illness? It was the bystanders who, with the certainty of ignorance ('knowing that she was dead') laughed to scorn the declaration of him who really knew that 'The maid is not dead but sleepeth.' He used similar language in reference to Lazarus, and it was only when he found it necessary to speak down to the comprehension of his disciples that he said 'Lazarus is dead.' Should we have any hesitation in saying that this, and the cases of the lad of Zarephath, of the body thrown into Elisha's tomb, of the young man of Nain and of Dorcas, were instances of conditions simulating death, probably catalepsy? (pp. 19–20)

We are now in a position to approach the question whether Jesus really died upon the cross. Taking the Gospel accounts as they stand, there is an entire absence of all the criteria which distinguished actual from apparent death. There was a hurried depositing in the sepulchre within three hours of the collapse upon the cross. There was no medical autopsy, no stethoscope test, no inquest with the evidence of those who had last to do with him. We have no account from Joseph of Arimathea who placed him in his tomb; none from Nicodemus who is said to have been with Joseph and to have supplied the usual burial spices and ointment; none from the gardener who under the circumstances might have been a material witness... (p. 20)

There is no statement as to when he left the tomb. He was first seen by a person unconnected with the burial, early on the third morning. Should anyone be misled by the expression, 'burial' into supposing that there was an internment and that consequently even if he were still alive when buried he must soon have been suffocated; it must be pointed out that the sepulchre was a rock-hewn chamber of considerable size, the entrance closed by a circular slab of stone, like a huge grind-stone, rolling in a grove in front of the opening, and not likely to hermetically seal the chamber. But it is quite consistent with the accounts that he revived under the treatment of Joseph and Nicodemus the first night... (p. 21)

Dr. Sparrow Simpson goes too far when he says (p. 47) [in *The Resurrection and Modern Thought*]:

'Believing, as we do, that all the evidence concurs in declaring that the grave was vacant, the interpretation of the fact must be ultimately one of two things: either this was a human work, or else it was the work of God. Either human hands removed the corpse or the Almighty raised the dead. That is exactly the question.' I venture to submit that is not the question. What if the supposed corpse was not really dead, and revived? I confidently submit that this interpretation of the vacant grave is ample and satisfactory. It postulates neither fraud nor miracle. (p. 25)

Going back to the discovery of returning animation, as suggested above, what might we reasonably conjecture would be the course of events? Before the revived Jesus could be removed from the tomb some clothing must be procured. If the gardener was assisting in the burial arrangements would it not be natural for him to run to his cottage, probably situated in the garden or near at hand, for his holiday garment to supply the need? If he was not of the party, still the gardener's cottage would be the most

CHAPTER THREE—THE STORY OF THE RESURRECTION   43

> likely place to send to for the clothes in the emergency. As soon as Jesus was sufficiently recovered, he would be removed from the tomb to the cottage till he could be conveyed to a place of safety. So he would probably be within the precincts of the garden when Mary Magdalene and the other woman came early in the morning. They receive a message perhaps from the gardener or his assistant (afterwards converted by the growth of legend into an angel or two) telling them of the rising and his intention to return to Galilee. They would also have opportunity for seeing Him themselves—being known as his friends. (pp. 32–33)

The author goes on:

> ... and if a solitary individual here and there ventured to raise his voice in dissent (to what the majority believed, namely, that Jesus did die upon the cross) it was drowned in the shouting of the multitude. There have even been periods in the history of the Church when such a person would run a grave risk of being roasted to death, not as a martyr, but as a heretic. (pp. 34–35)

The author then discusses whether Jesus went to Galilee whence he went to Damascus and appeared to St. Paul, after which he proceeded towards Babylon on his way to the East. Finally the author expresses his own belief in these words:

> For myself, I am content to believe that being man, he passed through the same gate—'The strait and

dreadful pass of death' that all others of human kind must go through... (p. 70)

He concludes his book with these words (pp. 77–78):

> ... I must repeat that we do not know [where he died]. It may be that after preaching to the lost tribes of the House of Israel in those remote regions, Jesus died at Srinagar, and was buried in the tomb that now bears his name. It may be that he never left his Galilean refuge, but suffered a lingering death from his wounds at his lonely camp fire by the Tiberian Lake, or on some solitary mountain summit, or in some secluded valley, and that 'no man knoweth of His sepulchre until this day.' We do not know; and perhaps it is as well that we do not. The Church has, at least, been preserved from relic worship of his bones; and to His unknown resting place we may address the closing lines of Mrs. Alexander's beautiful poem on the Burial of Moses:

'Oh lonely tomb!...
  Speak to these curious hearts of ours
And teach them to be still,
  God hath His mysteries of Grace,
Ways that we cannot tell;
  He hides them deep, like the secret sleep
Of him He loves so well.'

CHAPTER FOUR—
EARLY DOCUMENTARY EVIDENCE

In 1907 The Chicago Indo-American Book Co. published a book under the title 'The Crucifixion by an Eye-Witness'. This book contained a letter discovered in Alexandria in a house owned and occupied by the order of 'Essenes'. The letter was written only seven years after crucifixion by an highly esteemed member of the 'Essenes' brotherhood in Jerusalem to his brethren in Alexandria. It was written in reply to a letter from the leader of 'Terapeut' of Essenes Brotherhood in Alexandria who desired to know the real truth about the rumour that reached them relating to Jesus and his martyrdom, as they knew that he was their brother and lived in accordance with their rules.

The letter proves that Jesus belonged to the 'Essene Brotherhood'. The author of the letter assured his brethren in Alexandria saying:

I tell you only of the things I know and I have seen it all with mine own eyes and have taken a deep interest and an active part in all these transactions. (p. 38–39)

Darkness Descends on Earth

He tells us what happened when Jesus was put on the cross and when he was taken down. The letter says that while Jesus was on the cross;

Darkness descended over the earth, and the people returned to Jerusalem. (p. 62)

Continuing it says:

Jesus called out loudly, in the anguish of his pain, citing the twenty-second Psalm, praying God thereby to deliver him from his sufferings. (p. 62)

The Earthquakes

Proceeding, the letter says:

The heat grew steadily more intense, more unendurable, and a fire was forming in the earth and air, such as is essential to the purification of the elements. The Esseen brethren, through their knowledge of nature and its elements,

CHAPTER FOUR—EARLY DOCUMENTARY EVIDENCE 47

knew that an earthquake was coming, as had formerly occurred in the days of our forefathers. (p. 63)

As the night approached the earth began a terrible shaking, and the Roman Centurion became so terrified that he prayed to his heathen gods. Most of the frightened people hastily departed from the place and returned to Jerusalem; and the centurion, who was a noble man of compassionate nature, permitted John to conduct the mother of Jesus close to the Cross. (p. 63–64)

As he recommended his mother to the care of John, it was growing darker, although the full moon should have been shining in the heavens. From the Dead Sea was observed to rise a thick, reddish fog. The mountain ridges round about Jerusalem shook violently, and the head of Jesus sank down upon his breast. (p. 64)

When he uttered his last groan of anguish and pain, and passed away, a hissing sound was heard in the air; and they of the Jews were seized by a great fear, for they believed that the evil spirits who dwell between heaven and earth were proceeding to punish the people. It was that strange and unusual sound in the air that precedes an earthquake... (p. 64–65)

And as the Jews regarded all this as extremely supernatural, so the Roman Centurion believed now in the divinity and innocence of Christ, and comforted his mother... (p. 65)

Dear Brethren, you have reproached us, in that we did not save our Friend from the Cross by secret means. But I need only to remind you that the sacred law of our order prohibits us from proceeding publicly, and from interfering in matters of state. (p. 65–66)

Joseph and Nicodemus

The letter, enlarging on the part played by Joseph of Arimathea rendering aid to Jesus, says:

> There was a certain Joseph, from Arimathea. He was rich, and being a member of the council, he was much esteemed by the people. He was a prudent man, and whilst he did not appear to belong to any party, he was secretly a member of our sacred order and lived in accordance with our laws. His friend Nicodemus was a most learned man, and belonged to the highest degree of our order. He knew the secrets of the 'Terapeuts' and was often together with us. (p. 66)
>
> ... after the earthquake, and many of the people had gone away, Joseph and Nicodemus arrived at the Cross. They were informed of the death of the crucified, in the garden of our brethren not far from the Calvary. (p. 67)
>
> ... it ... appeared strange to them that Jesus, having hung less than seven hours, should already be dead. They could not believe it, and hastily went up to the place. There they found John alone... (p. 67)
>
> Joseph and Nicodemus examined the body of Jesus, and Nicodemus, greatly moved, drew Joseph aside and

CHAPTER FOUR—EARLY DOCUMENTARY EVIDENCE 49

> said to him: 'As sure as is my knowledge of life and nature, so sure is it possible to save him.' (p. 67)
>
> Nicodemus shouted: 'We must immediately have the body with its bones unbroken, because he may still be saved'; then, realizing his want of caution, he continued in a whisper, 'saved from being infamously buried.' (p. 68)

They kept it secret and did tell nothing to John about it.

> He persuaded Joseph to disregard his own interest, that he might save their Friend by going immediately to Pilatus, and prevailing upon him to permit them to take Jesus' body from the Cross that very night and put it in the sepulchre, hewn in the rock close by, and which belonged to Joseph.
>
> I, understanding what he meant, remained with John to watch the Cross and prevent the soldiers from breaking the bones of Jesus. (p. 68)
>
> The Jewish council had already demanded of Pilate an order to the soldiers to break the bones of the crucified, that they might be buried. (p. 68–69)

The letter further says that soon after Joseph and Nicodemus had departed, a messenger brought the order to the centurion to take down the corpses and bury them. The author of the letter says:

> As the messenger arrived I hastened to him, thinking and hoping that Joseph already might have seen Pilate, a thing of which there in reality was no possibility. (p. 69)

'Does Pilate send you?'... 'I come not from Pilate, but from the Secretary, who acts for the governor in such unimportant matters.' (p. 69–70)

The Centurion observing my anxiety, looked at me, and in the manner of a friend I said to him: 'You have seen that this man that is crucified is an uncommon man. Do not maltreat him, for a rich man among the people is now with Pilate to offer him money for the corpse, that he may give it decent burial.'

My dear Brethren, I must here inform you that Pilate often did sell the bodies of the crucified to their friends, that they might thus bury them.

And the Centurion was friendly to me, inasmuch as he had conceived from the events that Jesus was an innocent man. And therefore, when the two thieves were beaten by the soldiers with heavy clubs and their bones broken, the centurion went past the cross of Jesus, saying to the soldiers: 'Do not break his bones, for he is dead.' (p. 70)

Soon after this a messenger from Pilate came to the centurion and said that:

... Pilate desired to know if Jesus was indeed dead.

'So he is,' said the Centurion; 'therefore we have not broken his bones.'

To be the more sure of it, one of the soldiers struck his spear into the body in such manner that it passed over the hip and into the side. The body showed no convulsions, and this was taken by the centurion as a sure sign that he actually was dead; and he hurriedly went away to make his report.

But from the insignificant wound flowed blood and water, at which John wondered, and my own hope revived. (p. 71)

Pilate Hands over the Body

Speaking of the successful pleading of Joseph and Nicodemus to Pilate, the letter records:—

> ... Joseph and Nicodemus returned in great haste. Joseph through his dignity had moved Pilate, and Pilate, having received information as to the death of the crucified, gave the body to Joseph, and without taking pay therefor. (p. 72)
>
> For Pilate had a great reverence for Joseph, and secretly repented of the execution. When Nicodemus saw the wound, flowing with water and blood, his eyes were animated with new hope, and he spoke encouragingly, foreseeing what was to happen. (p. 72–73)
>
> He drew Joseph aside to where I stood, some distance from John, and spoke in a low, hurried tone: 'Dear friends, be of good cheer, and let us to work. Jesus is not dead. He seems so only because his strength is gone.'
>
> 'While Joseph was with Pilate I hurried over to our colony and fetched the herbs that are useful in such cases. But I admonish you that you tell not John that we hope to

reanimate the body of Jesus, lest he could not conceal his great joy. And dangerous indeed would it be if the people should come to know it, for our enemies would then put us all to death with him.' (p. 73)

Jesus Healed

The letter next dwells on the measures taken to revive and treat Jesus.

> After this they hurried to the cross, and, according to the prescription of the medical art, they slowly untied his bonds, drew the spike out from his hands, and with great care laid him on the ground. (p. 73)
>
> Thereupon, Nicodemus spread strong spices and healing salves on long pieces of 'byssus' which he had brought, and whose use was known only in our Order. (p. 73–74)
>
> These he wound about Jesus' body, pretending that he did so to keep the body from decaying until after the feast, when he would then embalm it.
>
> These spices and salves had great healing powers, and were used by our Esseer Brethren who knew the rules of medical science for the restoration to consciousness of those in a state of death-like fainting. And even as Joseph and Nicodemus were bending over his face and their tears fell upon him, they blew into him their own breath, and warmed his temples. (p. 74)
>
> The body was then laid in the sepulchre made in the

rocks, which belonged to Joseph. They then smoked the grotto with aloe and other strengthening herbs, and while the body lay upon the bed of moss, still stiff and inanimate, they placed a large stone in front of the entrance that the vapours might better fill the grotto. (p. 75)

Suspicions of Jews

The letter further tells us that Caiaphas the high priest of the Jews, who was anxious to know who were the secret friends of Jesus, sent out his secret spies. He suspected Pilate for his having given Joseph of Arimathea the body without any pay. Joseph who never took any interest in the case of Jesus previously but who now had given his own place of burial for the crucified. (p. 76)

Caiaphas knowing that they intend to embalm the body hoping to discover some secret means of accusing Joseph and having him thrown into prison he sent late in the night a number of his armed servants to an obscure valley close by the grotto in which lay the body of Jesus. (p. 75)

The writer of the letter further says:

> Meanwhile Nicodemus had hastened with me to our brethren, and the oldest and wisest came to confer as to the best means of restoring Jesus to life. And the brethren agreed immediately to send a guard to the grave.
>
> After midnight, and towards morning, the earth again commenced to shake, and the air became very oppressive. The rocks shook and cracked. Red flames burst forth from

the crevices, illuminating the red mists of the morning. (p. 77)

This was indeed, a dreadful night. Beasts, horrified by the earthquake, ran howling and crying in every direction ... the servants of the high-priest were full of fear, listening to the hissing in the air and the roaring and rumbling in the earth. (p. 77)

One of our brethren went to the grave, in obedience to the order of the Brotherhood, dressed in the white robe of the fourth degree. He went by way of a secret path which ran through the mountain to the grave, and which was known only to the Order. (p. 77–78)

When the timid servants of the high priest saw the white-robed Brother on the mountain slowly approaching, and partially obscured by the morning mist, they were seized with a great fear, and they thought that an angel was descending from the mountain.

When this Brother arrived at the grave which he was to guard, he rested on the stone which he had pulled from the entrance according to his orders; whereupon the soldiers fled and spread the report that an angel had driven them away. (p. 78)

Inside the Sepulchre

The author next records what was going on inside the grave where they had consigned the body of Jesus.

Thirty hours had now passed since the assumed death of Jesus. And when the Brother, having heard a slight noise within the grotto, went in to observe what had happened, he observed with inexpressible joy that the lips of the body moved, and that it breathed. He at once hastened to Jesus to assist him, and heard slight sounds rising from his breast. The face assumed a living appearance, and the eyes opened and in astonishment gazed at the novice of our Order.

This occurred just as I was leaving with the brethren of the first degree, from the council, with Joseph, who had come to consult how to bring help. (p. 79)

Nicodemus who was an experienced physician, said, on the way, that the peculiar condition of the atmosphere caused by the revolution of the elements was beneficial to Jesus, and that he never had believed that Jesus really was dead. And he further said the blood and water which flowed from the wound was a sure sign that life was not extinct.

Conversing thus, we arrived at the grotto, Joseph and Nicodemus going before. We were in all twenty-four brethren of the first degree.

Entering we perceived the white-robed novice kneeling upon the Moss-strewn floor of the grotto, supporting the head of the revived Jesus on his breast.

And as Jesus recognised his Esseer friends, his eyes sparkled with joy; his cheeks were tinted with a faint red, and he sat up, asking: 'Where am I?'

Then Joseph embraced him, folded him in his arms,

told him how it all had come to pass, and how he was saved from actual death by a profound fainting fit, which the soldiers on Calvary had thought was death. (p. 79–80)

And Jesus wondered, and felt on himself; and, praising God, he wept on the breast of Joseph. Then Nicodemus urged his friend to take some refreshments, and he ate some dates and some bread dipped in honey. And Nicodemus gave wine to drink, after which Jesus was greatly refreshed, so that he raised himself up.

Then it was that he became conscious of the wounds in his hands and in his side. But the balsam which Nicodemus had spread upon them had a soothing effect, and they had already commenced to heal. (p. 80–81)

Jesus Escapes the Sepulchre

The letter relates further how Jesus was spirited away from the grave. It says:

After the 'byssus' wrappings had been taken off and the muckender was removed from his head, Joseph spoke and said: 'This is not a place in which to remain longer, for here the enemies might easily discover our secret, and betray us.'

But Jesus was not yet strong enough to walk far, wherefore he was conducted to the house belonging to our Order, that is close by Calvary, in the garden, which also belongs to our brethren. (p. 81)

Another young Brother of our Order was dispatched at once to assist the novice who had been watching by the grave of Jesus, to annihilate every trace of the byssus wrappings and the medicines and drugs used.

When Jesus arrived at the house of our brethren he was faint and weak. His wounds had begun to cause him pain. He was much moved, in that he considered it all as a miracle.

'God has let me rise,' he said, 'that he may prove in me that which I have taught, and I will show my disciples that I do live.' (p. 81–82)

Jesus Meets Disciples

The letter further tells us that Esseer friends took all precaution and care for his safety and helped him by all means so that he was able to meet his disciples in Jerusalem, the valley at Messeda, in the house of Lazarus in Bethania, Galilee and Mount Karmel and other places, and deliver speeches to strengthen them in their belief and work. His speeches and talks, and the news that he was still alive caused a great stir amongst the people.

Jews Alarmed

It is clear from the letter that the suspicions of Jews that Jesus had survived the cross, were confirmed and they renewed efforts to liquidate him. The letter says in this connection.

> In the evening of the same day came Nicodemus to our Brotherhood and brought to us the information that Joseph of Arimathea had been arrested, and that they falsely attributed to him criminal purposes, in that he had been in secret association with Jesus. (p. 109–110)

Joseph was liberated afterwards from prison by the efforts of the holy Brotherhood in Jerusalem.

When Jesus was in the valley of Mount Karmel:

> ... the brethren warned Jesus of his danger, that he might avoid his enemies and thus fulfil his mission. For they had been secretly informed that Caiaphas intended quietly to arrest and assassinate Jesus, in that he believed him to be a deceiver. (p. 118)
>
> And Joseph spoke to Jesus saying:
>
> 'Knowest thou that the people who do not altogether understand your doctrine, are meditating to proclaim you worldly king, to overthrow the Romans? But thou must not disturb the kingdom of God through war and revolution. Therefore choose the solitude. Live with the Esseer friends and be in safety, that your doctrine may be proclaimed by your disciples.' (p. 120)

And Jesus consented that he would go into solitude.

Jesus Self-Exiled

The letter further tells us that the last time when Jesus met his disciples he:

> ... led them to the place most dear to him, near the summit of Mount Olivet, where can be seen almost the whole of the land of Palestine; for Jesus longed once more to look upon the country where he had lived and worked. (p. 123)
>
> ... And the chosen disciples believed that Jesus would lead them to Bethania. But the elders of the Brotherhood had silently come together on the other side of the mountain, ready to travel, waiting with Jesus, as had been agreed upon.
>
> And he exhorted his disciples to be of good cheer, and firm in their faith...
>
> He prayed for the friends he was about to leave, and lifting his arms he blessed them. And the mist rose around the mountain, tinted by the descending sun.
>
> Then the elders of the Esseer Brotherhood sent word to Jesus that they were waiting, and that it was then already late.
>
> As the disciples knelt down, their faces bent toward the ground, Jesus rose and hastily went away through the gathering mist. When the disciples rose there stood before them two of our brethren in white garb of our Brotherhood, and they instructed them not to wait for Jesus, as he was gone, whereupon they hastened away down the mountain. (p. 123–124)

> But the disappearance of Jesus filled his disciples with new hope and confidence, for now they knew that they themselves were to proclaim the word of Jesus, as he, their beloved, would return no more.
>
> ... But in the city there arose a rumour that Jesus was taken up in a cloud, and had gone to heaven. This was invented by the people who had not been present when Jesus departed. The disciples did not contradict this rumour, inasmuch as it served to strengthen their doctrine, and influenced the people who wanted a miracle in order to believe in him. (p. 125)

Dead to the World

The concluding part of the letter refers significantly to a plan adopted to set suspicions of the Jews at rest and to ensure the safe flight of Jesus from his own country to a foreign land.

The closing words of the letter about Jesus purport to show that only Joseph and Nicodemus had three times been with him in his place of concealment.

> ... the last time when the sixth full moon was waning, and they came to our Brotherhood... (p. 127–128)
>
> ... their hearts were sorely grieved, for the chosen one was taken up into the heavenly dwellings of the Father...
>
> And he was buried by the physician close by the Dead Sea... (p. 128)

The Esseer Brotherhood, according to the letter, told Jesus when he insisted on going among the people to tell them that God had saved him.

> ... 'Thou art not safe in this country, for they will search after thee. Do not, therefore, go any more among the people to teach, for what thou hast taught will live among thy friends for ever, and thy disciples will publish it to the world. Remain, I pray thee, dead to the world ... Live in the seclusion of wisdom and virtue, unknown to the world...' (p. 91–92)

The circumstances endorsed the wisdom of the aforesaid plan. It was accordingly decided that Jesus should remain 'dead to the world'.

It appears from the letter that Jesus' death and his burial were not seen by the author himself, and it was hearsay only, which was presumably made known by Joseph and Nicodemus as planned that Jesus should remain 'dead to the world' so that his opponents make no search for him. And if this statement about the death and burial of Jesus would have been factually true, at least some traces of his grave would have been found in the vicinity of the Dead Sea during the past centuries. At any rate, it is crystal clear from the letter under reference that Jesus did not die on the cross.

Comments of the German Translator

In his closing remarks, the German translator says:

... this letter contains so many interesting events, singularly corresponding with the account of the gospel, and recorded without any apparent motive of the author, in a pious, simple and in no way excited manner. (p. 133)

... But of particular importance is the minute record of the sufferings of Jesus, and the way in which he conducted himself on the cross. The gospel records that Jesus really died on the cross, and thereby it stamps his recovery as a miracle, which the intelligent man considers a myth, and from which he extracts the allegorical meaning. But in this letter we are informed of events in their simple representation that contains so much that is probable, and with the circumstances corresponding, that it actually will be a necessity to believe on it. (p. 140)

In the old letter is recorded that he did not die on the cross, but passed into unconsciousness. Even the way in which Jesus appeared to die on the cross makes the probability of apparent death possible. First, he lost consciousness very early, so that even Pilate doubted his death. Secondly, by the then existing mode of crucifixion, was it not uncommon that the crucified could be brought to life. (p. 141)

We are also informed by the historians of that date that it was not an uncommon thing that crucified criminals were brought back to life after being taken down from the cross. It is also proved that these unfortunates, among nations that did not have the Jewish custom of not allowing the crucified to hang on the cross over night, often would hang on the cross eight or nine days before death at last put an end to their dreadful sufferings.

When we examine into the methods of the crucifixion as it was executed on Jesus, we will be convinced that it could not be impossible for life to remain for a long time. (p. 141–142)

CHAPTER FIVE—
RECENT DISCOVERY:
SHROUD OF JESUS

German Scientists Make a Startling Discovery

The cloth, in which the body of Jesus was wrapped up, was found in the sepulchre (John xx:5). This cloth is still in existence. It bears the marks of the body of Jesus made by the ointment which was applied to his body.

Recently a group of German scientists have made some important revelations regarding this winding sheet of Jesus. They have shown that Jesus Christ did not die on the cross. He was taken down alive in a state of deep swoon or complete anaesthesia. By the time Mary Magdalene went to the sepulchre, he had recovered and disguised himself as a gardener to avoid re-arrest. His re-appearance on the earth was, therefore, not a resurrection, but recovery from a swoon.

The Scandinavian paper, *Stockholm Tidiningen*, published a leading article by the editor, Christer Iderlumd, on the subject in its issue of April 2, 1957. An Urdu translation of the same was published by the Sadr Anjuman Ahmadiyya, Rabwah (Pakistan), under the title, *Hazrat Masih Naseri Saleeb Par Hargiz Faut Naheen Hu'ay*. I am taking the liberty of rendering it into English as follows:

Did Christ Die on the Cross?

A group of German scientists had been making investigations regarding the shroud of Jesus for the last eight years. The results of their researches have been recently made available to the press. The two thousand year old winding sheet of Christ has been found in the Italian town of Turin. It bears the impressions of Christ's body.

The scientists have informed the Pope about the discovery. But the Pope is silent. The discovery brings to light a vital secret of the religious history of the Catholic Church. With the help of the art of photography, the scientists have tried to prove that the resurrection, which was regarded as a miracle by the people for the past two thousand years, was in fact a natural physiological phenomenon. They have conclusively proved that Christ did not die on the cross.

The issue of Christ's shroud has been under discussion

for the last one thousand years. This cloth was sent to Constantinople in 438 A.D. by Queen Endoxi. It was originally found near the catacombs. It remained in Constantinople for seven hundred years. Finally De La Roche took it away with him after an attack on Constantinople. When the fire broke out, the cloth was in a silver box. As a result of the melting of silver it became slightly indistinct. But the marks of Christ's body were still visible.

The people of France earned a large sum of money by displaying this cloth. From France it was taken to Turin, and there it was taken out for exhibition after every thirty-three years. In 1898 A.D. an Italian advocate looked at the negative in the light of the sun, he was astounded to find that it bore an exact likeness to Christ. When the negative was printed, it showed the face of the man (Jesus) whom no one had seen for the past 1900 years.

In 1931 A.D., when the cloth was again displayed, Guisepe Enrie, a photographer, took another photograph of the cloth with the help of bulbs operating at 6,000 and 20,000 volts supply in the presence of an important dignitary of the Church. This photograph brought to light a sensational fact, and demonstrated for the second time what Pia had already shown. The picture bears an exact likeness to the fact and body contours which the Church, for the last two thousand years, has been describing as those of Christ.

When a man looks at the photograph which has been reproduced in the book *Das Linnen Kurt Berna Stultgart* by Hanas Naber Verlage, he can easily understand the reaction of the Church. Pope Pius IX remarked:

"This picture has not been made by any human hand."

The scientists declare that the cloth and history both confirm that it is the picture of Christ. The manufacture and texture of the cloth show that it is the sort of cloth which was found at Pompeii.

The double marks on the cloth show that one half of the cloth was wrapped around the body of Christ, and the other half was used to cover his head. The ointment applied to Christ's body, together with the heat of the body reproduced the impressions of Christ's body on the cloth. The fresh blood of Christ as absorbed into the cloth also left marks on it. The photograph clearly shows the marks made by the crown of thorns on the base of the head and the forehead of Christ, the swollen right cheek of Christ, the deep spear mark on the right side, the blood stains due to blood flowing from the wounds caused by nails, and the marks on the back caused by friction with cross. But the most astonishing fact is that in the negative, the two closed eyes of Christ seem as if they are open.

The photograph also reveals that the nails were not struck on the palms but on the hard joints of the wrists. Another thing which becomes clear is that the spear did not touch the heart of Christ. The Bible says that *Christ gave up the ghost*, but the scientists insist that the heart had not stopped functioning.

It is also observed that if Christ had remained lifeless on the cross for an hour, the blood would have coagulated and become dry, as such no blood marks would have been left on the cloth. But the fact that the blood was absorbed in the cloth shows that Christ was alive when he was taken down from the cross.

I may add here that this sensational discovery of the German scientists merely confirms what was stated by Holy Quran fourteen centuries ago. The Holy Quran declares that Jesus had not died on the cross:

> And their [Jews'] saying, 'We did kill the Messiah, Jesus, son of Mary, the Messenger of Allah; whereas, they slew him not nor killed him by crucifixion, but he was made to appear to them like *one crucified*; and those who differ therein are certainly in a state of doubt about it, they have no *definite* knowledge thereof, but only follow a conjecture, and they did not convert this *conjecture* into a certainty. (The Holy Quran with English Translation by Maulvi Sher Ali, Rabwah, Chapter 4, verse 158.)[1]

---

1. This article was written by Miss Ulfat Qazi and published in the *Review of Religions,* June 1958. (Author)

CHAPTER SIX—
MODERN MEDICAL OPINION

The theory that Jesus only swooned on the cross and recovered is an ancient one. In 1928 Maulvi A. R. Dard, then the editor of the *Review of Religions*, made a written enquiry from Christian missionaries, ecclesiastical scholars, and professors concerning this theory. The Christian missionaries' reply was that the swoon theory had been discarded. Others confessed ignorance on the point. The editor, after reproducing their answer, writes:

> It is abundantly clear from these answers that the theory has not at all been discarded. They admit, on the other hand, that it has been forcibly received in these days. The Bishop of Birmingham is unable to say whether the swoon theory has been practically discarded by all critical scholars. Canon Streeter says the idea is revived in "The Brook Kerith." And the Bishop of Durham, one of the most eminent and learned authorities of the Church of England,

has no hesitation in saying, "It is scarcely accurate to say that the swoon theory to account for the Gospel narratives of the resurrection of Christ, has been discarded. It is repeated in a work published only a week or two ago, *Paganism in our Christianity,* by A. Weigall."

Leaving aside the stalwart supporters of the theory like Paulus, Venturini, Bahrdut, and Schleiermacher[1], we may mention only two more important publications which have just appeared on the continent:

1. *Dog Jesus pa Korest?* by Dr. Hugo Toll (Stockholm).
2. *De Proces de Jesus* by M. Paul Roue (Paris).

Then there is the most important book, 'The Crucifixion of Jesus by an Eyewitness', published from Los Angeles in 1919, which gave the graphic narrative account of the whole.[2]

Below I reproduce from the same number of the *Review of Religions,* the opinion of Dr. Hugo Toll, an eminent medical authority of Sweden. He, as the editor of 'RR.' says, is 70 years of age (in 1929) and remained in charge of the Stockholm Hospital from 1897 to 1923. The learned doctor proves medically that Jesus did not die on the cross. The rendering of what Dr. Hugo Toll has written in his book *Dog Jesus pa Korset?* is as follows:

---

1. See *The Quest of the Historical Jesus,* by Albert Schweitzer, translated by W. Montgomery. London. 1910.
2. *Review of Religions* No. 9, 1928.

Crucifixion was very common long before the time of Jesus, and the Romans used it frequently. They would not kill their victims at once, and crucifixion was a slow torture. It was a popular amusement. No procedure was laid down for it, so the executioners could treat their victims just as they liked. Sometimes they only fastened them with ropes, sometimes only their hands. The victim suffered both physically and mentally and the worst thing was the infamy. They used to crucify only slaves and people of a very low standing, and also criminals, traitors, and agitators.

Jesus hung on the cross, most probably naked. At that time of the year it was cold (John 18:18). Before the crucifixion they offered Jesus something to drink. We do not quite know what it was; wine and gall, or wine and myrrh: when he had tasted thereof he would not drink (Matthew 27:35). When the throat is contracted through some agony, one cannot swallow. When people suffer mentally or physically they often ask for water, but they can't drink it. This can also be evidence of temporary neurasthenia. Matthew (27:50) says that Jesus cried 'With a loud voice' and gave up the ghost. (Emphasis is on 'loud'). The centurion paid attention to this fact. He knew, perhaps by experience, that people do not usually die by uttering a cry. While he cried aloud, Jesus must have had some force left in him. There are in John's narrative some incidents interesting to a doctor, for they are so realistic and so very characteristic of an attack of shock and collapse. The usual cause of fainting is that the blood goes away from the head, and the patient turns pale. If you lay him down, he will feel an agonising dryness in the throat and in the mouth, and he will stammer or cry only the word 'water'. A fit of fainting may change into death, and thus the dying person may have been crying for water, but usually a dying person does not ask for water. You can see how his lips are drying, sometimes he would swallow a spoonful of water should you offer it to him, perhaps because the dying person has no power to refuse (though most often he does not refuse it). The fainting person, however (after an insufferable feeling of thirst), begins to lose consciousness. The earth seems to disappear under him, and he has a sensation of flying. Now he will cry as farewell warning perhaps, 'I am dying.' But a dying person, totally exhausted by haemorrhage and torture, will only open his mouth and draw his breath; he will never use the dramatic words, 'I am dying.' And Jesus said these words, 'It is finished. I am dying.'

He prayed for the persecutors. He saw the robbers on their crosses before they had put him on his. Then he thinks of his own and of all men's liberation. Then he thinks of his mother, and her future, like a good son, so simple and natural. He had thought he was the Messiah, that he should build up the land of God. Perhaps he would bring it about by his suffering. He remembers a hymn by David, 'My God, my God, why hast thou forsaken me?' At last, distress and fainting force him to think of himself, 'Father, into thy hands I commend my spirit,' and finally he cries, 'Water, I am dying.' What did Jesus die of? In the Gospels it is said only that 'he gave up the ghost.' By this is meant that he died. The centurion thought the same; otherwise he would have broken his bones. People can die from a mere apparent nothing. They can die of fright and shock. But few people died through crucifixion. Eusebius has related scenes from the prosecution of Diocletianus, and he says that crucified persons died after several days from exhaustion, hunger, or attacks by birds of prey or other wild animals. The robbers who were crucified with Jesus were alive in the evening, and the soldiers had to club them. When Joseph told Pilate that Jesus was dead, he did not believe it. He questioned the centurion, as Pilate had experience in these things. Jesus could have died from exhaustion and haemorrhage, but it is not likely that he did.

If Jesus had been dead no blood would have come. John who relates this incident, knew perhaps, the importance of this phenomenon. Those who understood it later on dared not speak of it. Jesus had been scourged in the morning. We know that a strong irritation of the skin can provoke oedema and blisters. There is a watery exudate which penetrates the skin and forms small or big blisters. This is called: *Epanchments Traumatiques de serosite. De coloment de la peau.* One of the soldiers saw the blisters and scratched one of them, perhaps out of mischief, perhaps a bit unwary, so that he wounded Jesus, and blood and water came out. Now Jesus was apparently dead, unconscious. Poor ignorant men did not understand that Jesus was not dead. They seem to have buried him in a temporary tomb, 'here they laid him because the grave was so near.' 'Perhaps he had found a gardener's mantle which was dirty and ugly.' When she (Mary) does not recognise him he says imploringly: 'Mary,' a single word. But it shows his helplessness and loneliness. Then she will recognise him, she will kiss his hands; but he says: 'Don't touch me.' He was so aching all over from his wounds that she must not touch him.

When he says, 'I have not yet gone to my Father' he uses the very flowery language of the Orient. He meant, 'I am not dead yet', but he feels so broken and ill and unhappy that he feels as if he could die any hour, and he sends his best wishes to his brothers.

Is that not perfectly natural? He had suffered the meanest punishment they knew in those days. He was a condemned man and a pariah. He must not defile the land with his presence, and he dared not show himself in public lest his enemies find him again. He is so shy that he hides himself in the garden; and as he is walking along a lonely road to Emmaus, one day, he meets his disciples, but only for a little while. They dare not offer help, dare not walk with him for fear of detection. If the disciples had helped him back they would not have left him to go alone hungry and friendless. Through messengers he arranged to meet them in a lonely place.

He disappears now and then, and at last he left them for ever.

Once only (Matthew 28:18) he is talking in his high tone; 'I have been given all power in heaven and earth.' We doctors know what that is: we call it 'Dementia Paranoids'.

In the Orient there is a religious community founded on the faith that Jesus lived after crucifixion, walked afterwards towards India, and at last, under the name of Izza (Issa) settled down in Srinagar (the town of happiness), in the beautiful valley of Kashmir. There he is said to have lived till he was 120 years old, and he lies buried there. They say that his name is Yuz Asaf. The name of this community is according to *Enzuklopadie des Islam*, 1913, B, page 218, Ahmadiyya.

This free opinion of a very eminent medical authority of Sweden, given after a careful examination of the accounts of the Gospels should leave no doubt that Jesus did not die on the cross, and if he had been examined by any medical authority, when he was taken down from the cross, he would certainly have certified accordingly.

CHAPTER SEVEN—
DID JESUS ASCEND TO HEAVEN?

It is evident from the four accounts of the Gospel writers that Jesus came out of the sepulchre with his physical body. When the disciples thought him a spirit, he said: 'Behold my hands and my feet, that it is I myself: handle me, and see; for a spirit hath not flesh and bones, as ye see me have.' Then he asked them, 'Have ye here any meat?' And they gave him a piece of broiled fish and of a honeycomb. And he took it and did eat before them.[1] He met his disciples only in secret or in out of the way places for fear of being rearrested. He did not show himself to others, as Peter says: 'God.. shewed him openly; not to all the people, but unto witnesses chosen before of God, *even* to us who did eat and drink with him after he rose from the dead'.[2]

Had he risen from the dead or his body been converted or

---

1. Luke 24:39–43
2. The Acts 10:40–41

transformed into an astral body, he would have had no fear of being rearrested or of death, and would have shown himself to his opponents and proclaimed in the public meetings his escape, his victory over death. Moreover, he would have shown his love to his enemies by preaching to them so that they might have believed in him. But he took precautions for his safety because he was with his mortal body afraid of being recaptured and put to death.

The various authors in their commentary, under verse 39, chapter 24 of Luke, write:

> One of the chief heresies in the primitive church was that which taught, in direct contradiction to this and other passages, that Christ was only an appearance, or phantom, having no real body, and therefore enduring no real sufferings. This risen body of the Lord was the same [as that] in which he now sitteth at the right hand of God.[1]

He asked his disciples if they had anything to eat and he did eat before them: he walked the whole distance from Jerusalem to Galilee on foot, not on the main road, but by circuitous paths in order to evade pursuit, which he need not have done if he had been other than an earthly being.

---

1. The New Testament of Our Lord and Saviour Jesus Christ. According to the Authorized Version. With a Brief Commentary by various authors, vol. 1 (The Four Gospels). Fifth Edition, Society for Promoting Christian Knowledge, London, 1872, Under Luke XXIV, in notes on verse 39. [Publishers]

The Sudden Appearance

>...when the doors were shut where the disciples were assembled for fear of the Jews, came Jesus and stood in the midst...[1]

This statement also does not show that he rose with an astral body. The various authors in their commentary on verse 39, chapter 24, of Luke say: 'How a body, having flesh and bones, could pass into a room with closed doors, we know not.'

In my opinion the passage does not show that Jesus' appearance was an extraordinary one, a miracle, that he was not with his mortal body. By showing his hands and side to his disciples[2], he himself confirmed that he was in earthly mould, and they were glad to see him. This passage only reveals the fact that Jesus came to his disciples where they were assembled 'for fear of the Jews', probably in a dark, gloomy, mud-built cottage. Most probably Jesus entered that place at the same time as they. It is not incredible also that their host (as they were stranger in Jerusalem) or Essene friends of Jesus led him to the place from a secret door, for the place had many doors. Luke relating this event, has omitted the mention of the doors, which clearly shows that it is not an important part of the event. Otherwise, their supposition that they saw a spirit was too well founded; but Jesus himself denied and proved its falseness by showing his hands and side and by his

---

1. John 20:19
2. John 20:27

clear-cut statement that he was the same Jesus with his body of flesh and bones.

I had already written the above account of the sudden appearance of Jesus in a closed room, when I found Docker's book 'If Jesus did not Die upon the Cross?' in which he has given a similar explanation of this sudden appearance. He writes (p. 14–16):

> Some have supposed that his body, after crucifixion, was endowed with supernatural power, such as the power of passing through closed doors ... But there is really no ground for this supposition. The three earliest Evangelists carefully arranged, what details they give as to the appearance, so as to exclude the idea that what the observer saw was Spirit and not a natural body; and even St. John does not say explicitly that Jesus passed through a closed door. Taking the words he uses as literally correct, it is a reasonable explanation to say that Jesus must have remained in concealment in Jerusalem until his return to Galilee. It is expressly stated that he did not appear in public. Obviously if the authorities became aware that he was alive he would be rearrested and executed, and so St. John says that doors were shut 'for fear of the Jews'. The doors so shut would be the outer doors. The most likely place for such concealment would be the house of his friends, where he and his disciples were accustomed to assemble, where he could be supplied with food, where he could have his wounds attended to. The outer doors being shut would not prevent him from coming from another part of the house into the room where the disciples assembled.

He might even have been in the room before they came in unperceived until he came and stood in their midst.

It is from St. Luke's story of the journey to Emmaus that it has been supposed that the risen Jesus had power to become invisible. He 'vanished out of their sight' when he went out of the house. Dr. Arthur Wright goes so far as to assert that he was 'one moment at Emmaus and the next in Jerusalem. At one instant he is the world of sense, at another in the world of spirit' (Christ's claim, etc., *The Interpreter*, July, 1916, p. 385), apparently forgetting that, according to St. Luke's account, the two disciples left Emmaus after he died and arrived at the room in Jerusalem before him. It is difficult to believe that St. Luke meant anything more than that he went away quickly (having to return to Jerusalem) when it is remembered that the story is followed immediately by proofs which Jesus gave that his body was still flesh and bone and not spirit.

If it is true that he asked Thomas to put his finger in the print of his nails; if it is true that he said to his doubting disciples, 'Behold my hands and my feet, that it is I myself, handle me, and see; for a spirit hath not flesh and bones as ye see me have'[1]; if it is true that he ate in the presence of disciples; if it is true that he disguised himself as a gardener after leaving the sepulchre; if it is true that he walked the whole distance from Jerusalem to Galilee on foot; if it is true that he took every possible precaution against rearrest; it follows as clearly as day follows night that the statement that

---

1. Luke 24:39

he appeared suddenly in rooms whose doors were shut is not true in its literal sense and that his body was not an astral body, but a body made of flesh and bones. This also shows that the statement of the Evangelists that forty days or so after the tragic events of the crucifixion he was lifted up to heaven by a cloud is a myth (if it is taken literally), for, it being established that he was in his body of clay, it is foolish to say that a vapour cloud lifted him up to heaven. No cloud has the power to raise a body of clay; no mortal can soar to heaven. If he had assumed an astral body, where did his body of clay go? He did not leave it in the sepulchre and we have seen that it was with a body of clay that he moved about during the remaining days of his sojourn in his native land. To say that he ascended to heaven with his mortal body, as we have quoted above from the commentary by various authors, is absolutely contrary to the sayings of Jesus, for he said: 'No man hath ascended up to heaven but he that came down from heaven.'[1] It is obvious that he did not descend from heaven with his body of flesh and bones; therefore, he could not ascend to heaven with the same. To say that he, with his body of flesh and bones, sat on the right hand of God, a pure pagan notion, is so ridiculous that it does not require any refutation.

The passages upon which the ascension theory is based are not reliable. Matthew says nothing about the ascension; he merely states that after coming out from the sepulchre Jesus went to Galilee and met his disciples at a mountain which he had appointed for them.[2]

---

1. John 3:13
2. Matthew 28:16

Mark asserts that Jesus sent a message to his disciples telling them to meet him in Galilee, and then without any connection with what he has mentioned before and without giving details as to place he makes this statement:

> So then after the Lord had spoken unto them he was received up into heaven and sat at the right hand of God.[1]

The last sentence, 'and sat at the right hand of God', weakens the whole statement as it is not conceivable that the writer also went up to heaven and saw Jesus sitting on the right hand of God. The truth concerning the last twelve verses of Mark is that 'they were added (to the original account) later still, probably early in the second century, probably to take the place of the ending which had been lost, or which was regarded as defective'.[2] Mark's account therefore, cannot be taken as a basis for this dogma.

St. Luke's account is:

> He led them out as far as Bethany, and he lifted up his hands, and blessed them. And it came to pass that while he blessed them, he was parted from them and carried up into heaven.[3]

Thus, according to St. Luke, he became separated from his

---

1. Mark 16:19
2. *Encyclopaedia Britannica,* ed. II, vol. 17, p. 730
3. Luke 24:50–51

companions which is far from meaning that they saw him ascending to heaven.

Again we read in the Acts:

And when he had spoken these things, while they beheld, he was taken up, and a cloud received him out of their sight.[1]

Now to be hidden from sight does not mean that he went up into the sky. It is very possible that he went to the top of the mountain, and the peak being obscured by clouds or mist, he was hidden from them; then from the top of the mountain, he proceeded on his way down the other side, leaving the country for some other land where he would be safe from the enmity and machinations of the Jews.

John confirms this by saying that Jesus met his disciples for the last time at the sea of Tiberias, and said to Peter, 'Feed my sheep' and he also said, 'Follow me', and Peter saw the disciple whom Jesus loved following him.[2]

There is no doubt these last few lines of John clearly indicate that Jesus did not ascend to heaven, but migrated to another country.

It is clear, therefore, that the accounts of both Matthew and John support this theory very strongly, whilst both are silent regarding the ascension.

Mark's account concerning the ascension is an addition to the

---

1. The Acts 1:8
2. John 21:16–20

original account by some unknown person. Luke, who refers in a vague way to his ascending to heaven, was not present with the disciples when Jesus parted from them and bade them farewell. As further evidence of their incompetence as authorities, we find them disagreeing upon certain important points. Two usher him into the heavens from Bethany, and from the Mount of Olives, and a third from Jerusalem without fixing any place, and Matthew says that he went on to Galilee and met his disciples, and John says that he parted from disciples at Tiberias.

Weigal writes:

> Ascension is not mentioned in the earliest Christian writings, namely, the Epistles, nor apparently, was it referred to in the earliest Gospel, that of St. Mark, for the words, 'He was received up into heaven', are quite vague and are included in those last twelve verses of the book which are now recognised by practically all Biblical scholars as a much later addition. [1]

Further, he says:

> Such an Ascension into the sky was the usual end to the mythical legends of the lives of pagan gods, just as it was to the very legendary life of Elijah. The god Adonis, whose worship flourished in the lands in which Christianity grew up, was thought to have ascended into the sky in the presence of his followers after his resurrection, and similarly

---

1. Weigal—*Paganism in our Christianity*, pages 99–101.

Dionysos, Herakles, Hyacinth, Krishna, Mithra and other deities went up into heaven.

The conclusion at which we arrive is that it is wrong to base the theory of the Ascension on such insecure grounds.

CHAPTER EIGHT— DID JESUS DIE ON THE CROSS AND ASCEND TO HEAVEN?

How Did the Belief Arise

It is true, as we have proved in the previous chapters that Jesus was alive when he was taken down from the cross, then why did early Christians, such as Saints Paul and Peter, believe in his death on the cross? For it is apparent from their epistles that the main point of their preaching was his death on the cross and subsequent resurrection, as it is today in most Christian sects. Undoubtedly, it is necessary to describe the position at length. The disciples of Jesus forsook him and fled in panic when he was arrested, and they do not appear as spectators when he was taken down from the cross nor when he came out from the sepulchre. Although he did not make a public appearance for fear of a rearrest, he met his disciples in secret or in out-of-the-way places only. If he had not seen them again and assured them that he had escaped from death, their faith in his Messiahship might have been shaken and they might have turned back seeing that he whom they had taken for the Promised Messiah of the Jews had died an 'accursed' death. So he showed himself to them in order to re-establish their tottering faith. Indeed his escape from the jaws of death was a cogent proof in favour of his claim. It strengthened them much. After he left the country, bidding them farewell at the sea of Tiberias, as John says, they stood firm. They even tried to preach his claim to the Jews, but the Jews persecuted them. Some were killed outright and some stoned to death. The Jews refuted their claim, rebuked them, and mocked at them affirming that they had let their Messiah die an accursed death. The disciples of Jesus could not tell of his escape for fear of cruel persecution, so it is more than possible that they concealed the matter and replied that Jesus had risen from the dead, as the Jews had made it generally known that he had died, and added that he had ascended to heaven by which they then meant that he had gone to a safe place.[1]

---

1. The term 'heaven' was used for any high raised place, as for instance we read in Exodus 19—20 that the Lord came down upon Mount Sinai on the top of the mount and spoke to Moses. But in verse 22 of chapter 20, the word 'heaven' is used instead of the top of the mountain. Moreover, we read in Shab. 89a, Ex. R. 1X1: 'Before Moses ascended to Heaven he said that he would descend on the forenoon of the forty-first day' (Jewish Encyc. word Moses). And in Ex. 24–28 it is clearly stated that Moses went into the midst of the cloud and got him up into the mount, and Moses was in the Mount forty days and forty nights. Similarly, Jesus was taken up on top of the Mount of Olives, and a cloud received him out of their sight. As the disciples saw him going up at the top of the mount according to the aforesaid usage they said he went to heaven.

However, this reply could not satisfy the Jews. They had not seen him ascend to heaven. So they believed him to have died an 'accursed' death.

Moreover, their preaching, in accordance with the teachings of their Master, was confined to the Jews only. It is quite evident that it was not easy for the Jews to believe in Jesus on account of the lowly origin of his disciples, while Jesus himself could not convince them. On the other hand, they were debarred from spreading their faith amongst other nations, firstly because they knew the latter would not accept the Mosaic Law, and secondly because Jesus had prohibited them from preaching to the Gentiles. In these unpromising circumstances, there arose a man named Saul, well known afterwards as Paul, who, not being one of the Apostles, declared his right to apostlehood on account of a vision, knowing that otherwise his claim had little chance of being recognised.

The Vision of St. Paul

The vision he beheld is mentioned in the Acts, Chapters 9, 22 and 26. If we read the separate accounts carefully we find them full of contradictions.

1. As an example, we read in Chapter 9, verses 3–6: 'That a light from heaven shone round about him and he fell to earth and heard a voice saying unto him, Saul ... and meanwhile those who journeyed with him stood speechless, hearing a voice but seeing no man'; but in Chapter 22, verse 9, he says: 'And they

that were with me saw indeed the light and were afraid but they heard not the voice of him that spoke to me.'

2. In Chapters 9 and 22 he says that a great light shone round about him only, but in Chapter 26 he says that the light shone round about him and about those who journeyed with him.

3. In Chapter 9 we read that he only fell to the earth and the others stood speechless, but in Chapter 26, verse 14, he states that he and all his companions had fallen to the earth.

4. In Chapter 22 he states that upon his asking what he should do, Jesus replied, 'Arise and go into Damascus, and there it shall be told thee of all things which are appointed for thee to do.' When he reached Damascus one Ananias came to him and told him what he should do.

5. In Chapter 26, however, he mentions nothing about this. On the contrary, he says that Jesus Christ himself told him of all things which he should have to do.

With these contradictions in the vision upon which he based his claim to be an apostle, we are led to doubt its reliability. If we admit that he did see a vision, a mere vision cannot be a sound basis on which to found a claim to apostlehood. However, he embraced Christianity in Damascus and straight away began to preach in the synagogues, that Christ was the son of God, confounding the

Jews who dwelt at Damascus, proving that this is the very Christ. The Jews took counsel to kill him.[1]

Before this, when Stephen was stoned to death by the Jews, he was standing by, consenting to his death.[2] And there was a great persecution instituted against the Church at Jerusalem: and they were all scattered abroad except the Apostles.[3]

St. Paul Goes to the Gentiles

Thus, having experienced persecution at the hands of the Jews, their insistence in rejecting the claims of Jesus, and not content with the slow and unpromising progress of Christianity, he withdrew, to study his new position, to some secluded spot in the region south of Damascus called Arabia.[4]

His contemplation revealed to him an idea which had not occurred to even Jesus. It was that Christianity should be preached to Gentiles. Three years after his conversion, he paid his first visit to Jerusalem for the purpose of making the personal acquaintance of Peter.[5]

He attempted to join the band of Disciples, but they did not at first accept him. He met the Disciples through Barnabas and

---

1. The Acts 9:23
2. The Acts 22:20
3. The Acts 8:1
4. Gal. 1:17
5. Gal. 1:18

told them of his vision and assured them of his sincerity by boldly preaching in Jerusalem in the name of Jesus.

According to his epistle to Galatians he abode with Peter fifteen days only and he saw no other Disciple besides James.[1]

Up to this time all those scattered abroad in consequence of the persecution following the death of Stephen, had travelled as far as Phenice, Cyprus, and Antioch, preaching the word unto none but Jews only.[2]

By this time Paul had despaired of the conversion of the Jews. So he determined to preach openly to the Gentiles. Nevertheless this was against the teaching of Jesus; he had strictly prohibited his disciples, saying:

'Go not into the way of the Gentiles and into *any* city of the Samaritans enter ye not: But go rather to the lost sheep of the house of Israel.'[3] And also: 'I am not sent but unto the lost sheep of the house of Israel', and 'It is not meet to take the children's bread and cast it *to* dogs'[4, 5].

---

1. Gal. 1:19
2. The Acts 11:19
3. Matthew 10:5–6.
4. Matthew 15:24–26
5. There are many other passages in the Gospels which clearly show that Jesus was not sent but to the Israelites. For instance, Mary was told by the angel that Jesus shall be given 'the throne of his father David' (Luke 1:32) 'And he shall reign over the house of Jacob for ever' (Luke 1:33). Concerning Bethlehem, Matthew quotes 'out of thee shall come a Governor, that shall rule my people Israel' (2:6). The Sermon on the Mount was addressed only to the Israelites. Jesus Christ, in spite of the fact that the other nations were living side by side with the Jews in Palestine, never preached to them. He prophesied about his twelve

When the Disciples tried to dissuade him from preaching to the Gentiles, he claimed that Jesus himself commanded him in a vision, whilst staying in Jerusalem to do so in these words:

> Make haste, and get thee quickly out of Jerusalem: for they [the Jews] will not receive thy testimony concerning me... Depart: for I will send thee far hence unto the Gentiles.[1]

Despite being opposed by the Disciples, he continued preaching to the Gentiles and was successful in his mission. The Disciples, who were bitterly persecuted, eventually agreed with him that he should continue his work among the Gentiles and they would preach to the Israelites.[2]

---

disciples that when 'the Son of man shall sit on the throne of his glory, ye also shall sit upon twelve thrones, judging the twelve tribes of Israel'(Matt. 19:28). The proceedings of the ease of Jesus in Pilate's court is also a positive proof that his mission was confined to the Jews only. Pilate considered him 'the King of the Jews' (Matt. 27:11, 37) and not the king of all the nations. When Peter began to preach to the Gentiles and to eat with them, those who were of the circumcision contended with him and he, then, could not quote any saying or instruction of Jesus to justify his action, but related his own vision (The Acts ch. 11). This shows that passages such as, 'Go ye therefore, and teach all nations, baptising them in the name of the Father, and of the Son, and of the Holy Ghost' (Matt. 28:19) are later additions. The Disciples never baptised anyone in the name of these three persons. The word 'nation' in certain passages can be interpreted as 'tribe,' while in other such passages it has been used in connection with the second advent of Jesus, which is the advent of Ahmad of Qadian, the prophet sent by God to guide all nations to Islam, because Islam is a universal religion.

1. The Acts 22:18–21
2. Gal. 2:7–12

Abolishment of the Mosaic Law

He further realised that to ensure success amongst the Gentiles, the teaching propounded by Jesus and practised faithfully by him and his disciples must be modified. He saw that the ceremonies and rites of the Mosaic Law could never be accepted by those who were not Jews. With characteristic boldness, therefore, he declared the abolishment of the Law with all ceremonials and ordinances and gave a new direction to Christianity which became a complex of his own active imagination, Roman thought, and Greek philosophy. He says:

1. 'By the deeds of the law there shall no flesh be justified in his sight: for by the law *is* the knowledge of sin...Therefore we conclude that a man is justified by faith without the deeds of the law'.[1]

2. 'For sin shall not have dominion over you: for ye are not under the law.'[2]

3. 'I do not frustrate the grace of God: for if righteousness *come* by the law, then Christ is dead in vain.'[3]

---

1. Rom. 3:20–28
2. Rom. 6:14
3. Gal. 2:21

4. 'Knowing that a man is not justified by the works of the law, but by the faith of Jesus Christ.'[1]

5. 'Behold, I Paul, say unto you, that if ye be circumcised, Christ shall profit you nothing.'[2]

These teachings were quite different from the teachings of Jesus who, during his whole life, acted according to the Law. A short time before he was arrested by the Jews, he celebrated and ate the Passover with his disciples.[3]

He said to a leper whom he had cleansed from leprosy: 'Shew thyself to the priest, and offer for thy cleansing those things which Moses commanded, for a testimony unto them.'[4]

He further enjoined them to offer their gifts on the altar.[5] His disciples also acted according to the Law; the woman who came with Jesus to Jerusalem prepared spices and ointments and rested on the Sabbath day, according to the commandment.[6]

St. Paul, therefore, had neither command nor right to abolish or to modify the commandments of the Law. He was not the Messiah, nor Prophet, nor, even an apostle. What right had he, therefore, to say: 'If ye be circumcised Christ shall profit you

---

1. Gal. 2:16
2. Gal. 5:2
3. Mark 14:12–14
4. Mark 1:44
5. Matthew 5:24
6. Luke 23:56

nothing,' whilst Christ himself[1] and all the Apostles were circumcised. Again Jesus says: 'Think not that I am come to destroy the law or the prophets: I am not come to destroy, but to fulfil.'[2] 'And it is easier for heaven and earth to pass, than one tittle of the law to fail.'[3]

Paul's statement that a man is not justified by the works of the Law is entirely erroneous. Zacharias and his wife 'were both righteous before God, walking in all the commandments and ordinances of the Lord, blameless'.[4] The Apostles of Jesus did not hold the same belief. James, the brother of Jesus for instance, says:

> What *doth it* profit, my brethren, though a man say he hath faith, and have not works? Can faith, save him? If a brother or sister be naked, and destitute of daily food, and one of you say unto them, Depart in peace, be ye warmed and filled; notwithstanding ye give them not those things which are needful to the body; what *doth it* profit? Even so faith, if it hath not works, is dead, being alone...Ye see then how that by works a man is justified, and not by faith only...For as the body without the spirit is dead, so faith without works is dead also.[5]

Paul's teachings levelled against the Law were not observed in

---

1. Luke 2:21.
2. Matthew 5:17
3. Luke 16:17
4. Luke 1:6
5. James 2:14–26

silence by the Apostles and others. They were alarmed at the deviation, and some of them went from Judea to the centre of Paul's work and told the new converts that except by faithful obedience to the Law and scrupulous observance of its ordinances such as circumcision after the manner of Moses they could not be saved.[1] Consequently, great strife and dispute arose between them and Paul. It caused Paul to go with certain of his party to Jerusalem, where a meeting was convened to consider the matter and was attended by the Apostles, elders and other disciples.

Violent and hot discussions followed. Paul's work, by this time, had made decisive progress, and it was almost impossible for the Apostles to stop it. On the other hand, preachers to the Jews could not make any progress and were gradually despairing of any victory against Judaism. Under the influence of these two factors Peter rose and upheld the view of Paul. In the end, James made a speech, and concluded (Acts 15:19):

> Wherefore my sentence is, that we trouble not them, which from among the Gentiles are turned to God.

Finally, the following letter was written to them:

> The apostles and elders and brethren *send* greetings unto the brethren which are of the Gentiles in Antioch and Syria and Cilicia. Forasmuch as we have heard, that certain which went out from us have troubled you with words, subverting your souls, saying, *Ye must* be circumcised, and

---

1. The Acts 15:1

keep the law: to whom we gave no *such* commandment: ...For it seemed good to the Holy Ghost, and to us, to lay upon you no greater burden than these necessary things; that ye abstain from meats offered to idols, and from blood, and from things strangled, and from fornication.[1]

Christ as a Substitute for the Mosaic Law

When Paul saw his efforts crowned with success, through the agreement that he should preach to the Gentiles only without requiring from them the fulfilment of the Law, whilst the Jews would be bound to a minute observance of it, he again overstepped the limits set to his activities and preached the entire abolition of the Law not only for the Gentiles, but for the Jews as well, maintaining that faith in the blood of Jesus took its place.

Thus he says:

> The Law was our schoolmaster to bring us unto Christ that we might be justified by faith. But after that faith is come we are no longer under a schoolmaster.[2]

> A new covenant hath made the first old. Now that which decayeth and waxeth old is ready to vanish away.[3]

---

1. The Acts 15:23–29
2. Gal. 3:24, 25
3. Heb. 8:13

The disciples of Jesus, after he had bade them farewell, answered the mocking Jews, who asserted that they had caused their Messiah to die an 'accursed' death, that he rose from the dead. But his resurrection was difficult to prove. He made no public appearance and remained in hiding all the days he stayed there. When he migrated to another country they stated, metaphorically, that he had ascended to heaven. This answer was more incredible than the former and also unsatisfactory to the Jews who had thought that he had died an 'accursed' death.

When Paul proclaimed the abolition of the Law, and absolved the people from the necessity of complying with the Law, he boldly told the Jews that it was true, as they said, that Jesus died an accursed death, but to redeem us 'from the curse of the law, being made a curse for us, for it is written: Cursed is every one that hangeth on a tree.'[1]

Now the belief that sins are forgiven by the offering of gifts and sacrifices of animals was well established among the Jews. Thus, Micah, the prophet, says:

> Wherewith shall I come before the Lord, and bow myself before the high God? Shall I come before him with burnt offerings, with calves of a year old? Will the Lord be pleased with thousands of rams, or with ten thousands of rivers of oil? Shall I give my firstborn for my transgression, the fruit of my body for the sin of my soul?[2]

---

1. Gal. 3:13
2. Micah 6:6–7

Paul took this belief as a basis for the abolition of the Law and said:

> Neither by the blood of goats and calves, but [Jesus] by his own blood entered in once into the holy place, having obtained eternal redemption for us. For if the blood of bulls and of goats, and the ashes of an heifer sprinkling the unclean, sanctifieth to the purifying of the flesh: how much more shall the blood of Christ, who through the eternal Spirit offered himself without spot to God, purge your conscience from dead works to serve the living God?[1]

Again he says:

> [Jesus] in whom we have redemption through his blood, even the forgiveness of sins.[2]
>
> Christ died for our sins.[3]

As far as the Gentiles are concerned, they believed the same concerning their gods as I will show in the following chapter. Thus, Paul based his preaching to the Gentiles on the crucifixion and resurrection of Jesus saying that Jesus the Christ 'was raised from the dead according to my gospel'.[4]

---

1. Heb. 9:12–14
2. Coloss. 1:14
3. 1 Cor. 15:3. Also see Romans 5:8, 10
4. 2 Tim. 2:8

> And if Christ be not risen [from the dead], then *is* our preaching vain, and your faith *is* also vain.[1]

As Paul was a Roman[2] and from his journeys into Syria etc., knew the mentality of the Gentiles, he based his preaching on the pre-existing ideas of the Gentiles which they could easily assimilate.

It is evident from the New Testament that Paul did not see Jesus and that he was not present when Jesus was put on the cross, taken down, and came out of the sepulchre and bade farewell to his disciples. Three years after his conversion he came to Jerusalem and stayed with Peter for fifteen days. After fourteen years he came again to Jerusalem to convince the Apostles of the truth of the preaching.

The reason why Paul advanced the doctrine of the crucifixion and resurrection was but to convert the Gentiles by abolishing the Law, to redeem them from sin, and to absolve them from the ordinances of the Law. From among the Apostles who supported him and followed him, adopting his method of preaching, was Peter with whom he lived for fifteen days. We learn from the Gospels that Peter was inconsistent and wavering in his nature, and not very firm in his belief. We read in Matthew's Gospel that he told Jesus,

> Though all *men* shall be offended because of thee, *yet* will I never be offended.[3]

---

1. 1 Cor. 15:14
2. The Acts 22:25
3. Matthew 26:33

But shortly afterwards he thrice denied Jesus and with an oath said that he did not know him.¹

Paul himself bears witness that Peter was weak of faith. He says:

> But when Peter was come to Antioch, I withstood him to the face, because he was to be blamed. For before that certain came from James, who did eat with the Gentiles: but when they were come, he withdrew and separated himself, fearing them which were of the circumcision. And the other Jews dissembled likewise with him; insomuch that Barnabas also was carried away with their dissimulation. But when I saw that they walked not uprightly according to the truth of the gospel, I said unto Peter before *them* all, If thou, being a Jew, livest after the manner of the Gentiles, and not as do the Jews, why compellest thou the Gentiles to live as do the Jews?²

So is it not incredible if a man like Peter, under the influence of Paul, showed his belief in the blood of Jesus and preached against the teachings of his master, affecting to have seen a vision like Paul.

> And he [Peter] became very hungry, and would have eaten: but while they made ready, he fell into a trance, and saw heaven opened, and a certain vessel descending unto him, as it had been a great sheet knit at the four corners, and let

---

1. Matthew 26:72–75
2. Gal. 2:11–14

down to the earth: wherein were all manner of fourfooted beasts of the earth, and wild beasts, and creeping things, and fowls of the air. And there came a voice to him, Rise, Peter; kill, and eat. But Peter said, Not so, Lord; for I have never eaten anything that is common or unclean. And the voice *spake* unto him again the second time, What God hath cleansed, *that* call not thou common. This was done thrice: and the vessel was received up again into heaven.[1]

Had these people given any thought to this matter of visions they would have known that vision can be from Satan or the result of their own thoughts; a vision contrary to the word of God cannot proceed from Him. When God said to Moses that 'Swine... *is* unclean to you: ye shall not eat of their flesh',[2] then the voice heard by Peter that all beasts are clean certainly was the voice of the devil, not of God.

As for Paul, we cannot describe him more accurately than he has described himself. He says:

And unto the Jews I became as a Jew, that I might gain the Jews; to them that are under the law, as under the law, that I might gain them that are under the law; to them that are without law, as without law, ...that I might gain them that are without law.[3]

---

1. The Acts 10:10–16
2. Deut. 14:8
3. 1 Cor. 9:20–21

And he let the cat out of the bag by saying:

> For if the truth of God hath more abounded through my lie unto his glory; why yet am I also judged a sinner?[1]

This policy of Paul made him modify the teachings of Jesus and to claim what he could not do otherwise. In spite of not being an apostle he proclaimed himself one of the Apostles who lived with Jesus. Peter, as I have mentioned above, explicitly declared that Jesus, after his resurrection, did not show himself in public, but to the disciples only, and the four accounts of the Gospel writers testify the same. But Paul, to confirm his apostleship, contradicts them all, saying that Jesus was seen of Cephas, then of the twelve (whilst there were eleven only), then of above five hundred brethren, then of James, then of all the apostles. And last of all he was seen of me also.[2]

For the sake of the Gentiles, Paul and Peter, and those who followed them, changed the religion taught by Jesus. They believed in his crucifixion and resurrection and that he was 'accursed' to redeem them of their sins. They taught the people that it was sufficient for a man to believe in the blood of Jesus to obtain salvation. Gradually this easy religion, which should be called Paulinism, became more and more prominent till it swept away every vestige of the principles taught by the founder of what today is known as Christianity.

---

1. Rom. 3:7
2. 1 Corin. 15:6–9

CHAPTER NINE—
PAGANISM AND PAUL

Jesus, as I have mentioned in the last chapter, forbade his disciples to preach any people other than the Israelites. Concerning his mission he says:

> I am not sent but unto the lost sheep of the house of Israel.

Referring to other nations as dogs, he says:

> It is not meet to take the children's bread and cast it to the dogs.[1]

Throughout the ministry, Jesus preached to the Israelites only and likewise did his disciples. Had Jesus been sent to the Gentiles also, he would have preached to them too. They lived in Palestine side

---

1. Matt. 15:24, 26

by side with Jews. But he did not. A few passages of the Gospels such as 'teach all nations' in Matt. 28:19 which are set against the above saying of Jesus and his practice, are either additions by unknown persons or the word 'nation' means tribe and not nation (see Ency. Biblica). If the passage is connected with the second advent of Jesus, the prophecy has been fulfilled in the person of Ahmad (peace and the blessings of God be upon him), the founder of the Ahmadiyya Movement. I have written about this subject in my book, 'Islam'.

It was St. Paul who, contrary to the instructions of Jesus and the practice of his disciples, originated the idea of preaching to the Gentiles. It is beyond comprehension that Jesus himself and his companions who lived with him could not know the true mission of Jesus, and St. Paul, who never had the privilege of meeting or hearing him, should find the real mission for which he was sent. I do not think there can be anything more ridiculous than this. Jesus explicitly commanded his disciples:

Go not into the way of the Gentiles.[1]

But St. Paul, being annoyed with the Jews for their opposition, said:

I am clean: from henceforth I will go unto the Gentiles.[2]

---

1. Matt. 10:5
2. The Acts 18:6

The result of his overstepping the limits laid down by Jesus for preaching, was what Jesus had foretold, saying:

> Give not that which is holy to the dogs, neither cast ye your pearls before swine, lest they trample them under their feet, and turn again and rend you.[1]

When St. Paul began to preach to the Gentiles, the latter's attitude compelled him to modify the principles taught by Jesus. He presented the crucified Jesus in the way they believed in their gods. I mention below, by way of example, a few gods in which the Pagans believed.

1. At the festivals of Adonis, which were held in western Asia and in Greek lands, the death of the god was annually mourned with a bitter wailing, chiefly by women; images of him dressed to resemble corpses were carried out for burial and then thrown into the sea or into springs. In some places his revival was celebrated on the following day. At Alexandria they sorrowed not without hope, for they sang that the lost one would come back again. In the great Phoenician Sanctuary of Astarte at Byblus the death of Adonis was annually mourned—but next day he was believed to come to life again, and ascend to heaven in the presence of his worshippers.[2]

---

1. Matt. 7:6
2. Sir James Frazer Adonis, Attis. Osiris, edition 2, page 183–84 Macmillian & Co., Ltd., London, 1907.

2. *Hanged God.*—In olden days the priest who bore the name and played the part of Attis at the spring festival of Cybele, was regularly hanged or otherwise slain upon the sacred tree. This barbarous custom was afterwards mitigated into the form in which it is known to us in later times when the priest merely drew blood from his body under the tree and attached an effigy instead of himself to its trunk. In the holy grove at Upsale men and animals were sacrificed by being hanged upon the sacred trees. The human victims dedicated to Odin were regularly put to death by hanging or by a combination of hanging and stabbing, the men being strung up to a tree or a gallows and then wounded with a spear. Hence Odin was called the Lord of the gallows or the god of the hanged, and he is represented sitting under a gallow. Indeed he is said to have been sacrificed to himself in the ordinary way as we learn from the weird verses of the Havamal given below in which the god describes how he acquired his divine power by learning the magic:

> *I know that I hung on the windy tree*
>   *For nine whole nights;*
> *Wounded with the spear, dedicated to Odin, Myself to myself.*[1]

3. Arthur Weigall writes:

> One of the earliest seats of Christianity was Antioch, but in that city there was celebrated each year the death and resurrection of the god Tammuz or Adonis, the latter

---

1. do. p. 243, 244

name meaning simply 'the Lord'. The place at Bethlehem selected by the early Christians as the scene of the birth of Jesus (for want of any knowledge as to where the event had really occurred) was none other than an early shrine of this pagan god, as St. Jerome was horrified to discover, a fact which shows that Tammuz or Adonis ultimately became confused in men's minds with Jesus Christ. This god was believed to have suffered a cruel death, to have descended to Hell or Hades, to have risen again, and to have ascended into heaven: and at his festival, as held in various lands, his death was bewailed, an effigy of his dead body was prepared for burial by being washed with water and anointed, and on the next day, his resurrection was commemorated with great rejoicings, the very words, 'The Lord is risen' probably being used. The celebration of his ascension in the sight of his worshippers was the final act of the festival.[1]

There is one feature of the gospel story which seems really to have been borrowed from the Adonis religion, and in fact from other pagan religions also, namely, the descent to Hell.[2]

4. Another religion which had its influence on Christianity was the worship of the Spartan god or divine hero, Hyacinth, who

---

1. Weigall, *Paganism in our Christianity*, p. 110-111, Hutchinson & Co. Ltd., London.
2. do. p. 113

had been killed by an accidental blow. His three days' festival was held each year in spring or early summer. On the first day he was mourned as dead; on the second day his resurrection was celebrated with great rejoicings; and on the third day, it seems, that his ascension was commemorated, the sculptures at his tomb showing him ascending to heaven, with his virgin sister, in the company of angels or goddesses.[1]

5. Then again, there was the worship of Attis. Attis was the Good Shepherd, the son of Cybele, the Great Mother, alternatively, of the virgin Nana, who conceived him without union with mortal man, as in the story of the Virgin Mary; but in the prime of his manhood he mutilated himself and bled to death at the foot of his sacred pine tree. In Rome the festival of the death and resurrection was annually held from March 22nd to 25th. At this festival a pine tree was felled on March 22nd and to its trunk an effigy of the god was fastened. Attis thus being 'slain and hanged on a tree', in the Biblical phrase. This effigy was later buried in a tomb. March 24th was the Day of Blood, whereon the High Priest, who himself impersonated Attis, drew blood of a human sacrifice, thus, as it were, sacrificing himself. It recalls to mind the words in the Epistles of the Hebrews:

'Christ being come an High Priest...neither by the blood of goats and calves, but by his own blood...obtained eternal redemption for us.'

---

1. do. p. 155

That night the priests went to the tomb and found it illuminated from within, and it was then discovered to be empty the god having risen on the third day from the dead, and on the 25th the resurrection was celebrated with great rejoicings, a sacramental meal of some kind being taken, and initiates being baptised with blood whereby their sins were washed away and they were said to be born again.[1]

6. The central idea in the worship of Adonis was the death and resurrection of this god: he was killed by a boar, but the boar was an incarnation of himself, and thus the god was both executioner and victim, an idea propounded in the Epistle to the Hebrews wherein Christ is described as high Priest, who to put away sin, sacrificed Himself. Similarly Mithra sacrificed a bull, but this bull, again, was himself; a goat and a bull were sacrificed to Dionysos, but they were themselves aspects of that god; a bear was sacrificed to Artemis, but this bear, likewise was Artemis herself; and so forth. Thus the idea of a god atoning to himself for the sins of mankind by his own sacrifice was widespread; and human sacrifices in general directly or indirectly symbolising the beneficial deaths of gods, were matters of ordinary thought and conversation. Tertullian says that children were sacrificed to Saturn as late as the proconsulship of Tiberius. Dion Cassius speaks of the sacrifice of the two soldiers to Mars in the time of Julius Caesar, and other

---

1. do. p. 116–117

instances might be cited to show how general was the belief in the efficacy of human sacrifice in the time of Christ.[1]

The immemorial Jewish views as to sin-offering were firmly held in the time of Christ; and the sacrifice of a lamb, goat or some other animal for the remission of sins was a regular custom, and the scapegoat[a] which, bearing all the sins of the nation, was driven to the wilderness to be devoured by beasts of prey, was employed as a variant of this practice. On all sides the pagan gods were supposed to have suffered and bled for mankind, while their altars reeked with the blood of human and animal victims tortured and slain for the remission of sins.[3]

Sir James Frazer says:

The employment of a divine man or animal as a scapegoat is especially to be noted...Evils are believed to be transferred to a god who is afterwards slain...On one hand we have seen that it has been customary to kill the human or animal god in order to save his divine life from being weakened by the inroads of age. On the other hand, we have seen that it has been customary to have a general

---

1. do. p. 154–155

(a) The scapegoat is often quoted by fundamentalist Christians as a type of the sacrifice made by Jesus, forgetful of the fact that the scapegoat was not sacrificed but was sent into the wilderness *alive*. (Author)

3. do. p. 156–157

expulsion of evils and sins once a year. Now if it occurred to people to combine these two customs, the result would be the employment of the dying god as a scapegoat. He was killed, not originally to take away sin, but to save the divine life from the degeneracy of old age, but since he had to be killed at any rate people may have thought that they might as well seize the opportunity to lay upon him the burden of their sufferings and sins in order that he might bear it away with him to the unknown world beyond the grave.[1]

If these pagan beliefs are compared with the story of the crucified Jesus presented to the Gentiles by St. Paul, we would find that the latter is nothing but a copy of the former. As a matter of fact the disciples of Jesus did not lay stress on his crucifixion and resurrection, and we do not hear much of this novel doctrine until the return of Paul from Arabia when he began to preach to the Gentiles. The first martyr of Christianity was admittedly Stephen, whose martyrdom affected the mind of Paul very deeply. In the Acts, Chapters 6 and 7, we read an account of this great martyr. He 'did great wonders and miracles among the people'. Then he had a great discussion with the Jews. He denounced the local worship of the Holy Place of the Temple, and for his blasphemous word against Moses, and against God, he was arrested. Then he delivered an excellent and animated discourse on scriptural matters; but not a single word does he say about the 'resurrection'

---

1. Sir James Frazer. *Golden Bough,* Part 6 The Scapegoat, p. 226–7, London, 1913.

of Jesus throughout the long dispute. If the risen 'Lord' was the centre of his convictions, why did he not say so? In his speech he should have emphasised the 'resurrection' more than anything else. But it is not so.

It is Paul alone who lays stress on the crucified Jesus, and is enthusiastic about the 'resurrection'. As he says,

> If Christ be not risen, then *is* our preaching vain and your faith *is* also vain.[1]

And he it was who said:

> Christ hath redeemed us from the curse of the law, being made a curse for us.[2]

And he was who gloried in the Cross of Jesus Christ.[3]

The earliest group of disciples did not appreciate his innovation, they opposed him as far as they could but as time passed his easy religion, though rejected by the Jews, became the conquering religion of the pagan Roman Empire. The pagan beliefs and ceremonies were enacted, and the merging of the worship of Attis into that of Jesus was effected. And 'it was at the Council of Nicaea, in the year 325, about three centuries after the crucifixion, that Jesus was first recognised officially by the Church as God'.[4] Thus

---

1. 1 Cor. 15:14
2. Gal. 3:13
3. Gal. 6:14
4. *Paganism in our Christianity,* p. 168.

the doctrine originated by Paul resulted in the taking of Jesus, a mortal being as God; and yet he had been sent to establish the Oneness of God and to teach that no one should be worshipped besides Him!

Did Jesus Prophesy the Crucifixion and Resurrection?

In 1927, when I was in Damascus, a debate in writing took place between myself and Rev. Alfred Nelson, then in charge of the Christian Mission in Damascus, on the subject: 'Did Jesus die on the Cross?' During this he asked me the following question: 'If we believe that Jesus did not die on the cross, then was his prophecy that he would be killed and rise again on the third day untrue?'

My reply to this question was: You cannot say positively that these were the exact words spoken by Jesus. These books were written at a time when the theory of crucifixion, invented by Paul, had come to be accepted by the majority of the Christians.

Luke as we know, was very much in the company of Paul. He accompanied him on many of his travels.[1] He was with him at Rome.[2] And Mark, according to a fragment of Papias, was the follower and interpreter of Peter.[3]

Furthermore, it is in dispute who were the authors of the other two Gospels. It is not strange, therefore that we should find

---

1. See for instance the Acts 16:12 and 28:13.
2. 2 Tim. 4:11
3. Ency. Brit., edition II Vol. 17 p. 729.

some sentences in these books in support of Paul's theory. It must also be remembered that the words of this prophecy differ in each Gospel. Thus, Matthew says that when Jesus told his disciples that he would be betrayed into the hands of men and they would kill him, 'and the third day he should be raised again. And they were exceedingly sorry'.[1] This passage shows that they understood what he said and were sorry about it. Luke says that he told them that he would be delivered into the hands of men. 'But they understood not this saying and it was hid from them, that they perceived it not they feared to ask him of that saying.[2] And it appears from the fourth Gospel that they had no knowledge of any prophecy to the effect that he must rise again from the dead.[3] And Mark says that when Mary Magdalene told the Disciples, as they mourned and wept that Jesus was alive and had been seen of her, they disbelieved. After that he appeared unto two and when the two told the rest, neither did they believe. Then he appeared to the eleven and upbraided them with their unbelief and hardness of heart, because they believed not them which had seen him after he was risen.[4] Their lamentation and their disbelief in the news of his resurrection, show they had no knowledge of any prophecy of this kind.

Thirdly, it can be said that the second part of this prophecy: 'That he would be raised on the third day', was not fulfilled to the very words. According to John 20:1 and Luke 24:1, he was in the

---

1. Matt. 17:23
2. Luke 9–45 and Mark 9:32
3. John 20:9
4. Mark 16:10–14

sepulchre one day and two nights, and not three days and three nights as the prophet Jonas was in the belly of the whale. Neither was the first part of the prophecy fulfilled as to the very words, except that we may say that the semblance of death on the cross, as seen by John the Divine, that he saw him [i.e., the Lamb] 'as it had been slain'[1] is a symbolical reference to death, or that the terrible torture which he was going to suffer on the cross followed by a swoon is figuratively meant as death.

On the other hand, there are many prophecies, some of which I have mentioned in the first chapter, which show that God would save him from death on the cross. It is undeniable, therefore, that when everyone had despaired of his life, God saved him from death and thus was fulfilled what he had foretold. He remained in the sepulchre alive just as Jonah remained alive in the belly of the whale.

---

1. Rev. 5:6

CHAPTER TEN—
REDEMPTION OR ATONEMENT

It is evident from the last chapter that the pagans believed in the sacramental sufferings, death, and resurrection of their gods Adonis, Attis, Osiris, Mithra, etc., who had died 'for the sins of mankind'. Primitive and semi-civilised idolaters of various countries, especially West Africans, had many forms of sacrifice. In the annual 'customs' of Dahomey, now abolished, hundreds of human victims were sacrificed. Three main forms of human sacrifice existed in this area: (1) The scapegoat; (2) the messenger; and (3) the expiation, but combinations were not infrequent. The victim was oft kept in captivity and well fed; to transfer their sins people laid their hands upon him as he was led in procession, his head covered with ashes; on the way to the place of sacrifice were three enclosures, the second open to chief and priests only, the third to the official and his helper alone; the blood of the victim was offered to the gods.[1]

The idea of propitiatory sacrifice of animals was found in Judaism (probably borrowed from the pagans of Babylon), but they never believed in human sacrifice, not that the Messiah would be sacrificed on the cross as a ransom for the sins of the world.

Jesus himself never said anything which could be interpreted with certainty as meaning that the forgiveness of original or actual sin and a great reconciliation between God and man were to be the consequence of his death; he never said that his death was to be regarded as a sacrificial atonement. The words 'the Son of man came...to give his life a ransom for many'[2] are evidently a comment by the author of the Gospel, not the words of Jesus and, even if spoken by Jesus, they might only have meant that just as he had lived to bring happiness to others, so he was prepared to die alone for this cause without implicating his followers.

The words used by him at the Last Supper are usually supposed to indicate the sacrificial and atoning nature of his death but this is a misinterpretation. In the Gospel of St. Mark, Jesus says (14:24): 'This is my blood of the new testament, which is shed for many,' and in St. Luke he says (22:20): 'This cup *is* the new testament in my blood, which is shed for you,' and it is only in the much later Gospel of St. Matthew that the words 'for the remission of sins' are added (26:28). 'The most conservative critic,' wrote Hastings Rashdali, the Dean of Carlisle, 'will have no hesitation in treating

---

1. Ency. Britt. edition 11 Sacrifice
2. Mark 10:45

this addition as an explanatory gloss by the author of the Gospel,[1] and the meaning of the other words may well have been simply that he was about to lay down his life for his friends and to die for the cause.'[2] St. Paul and his collaborators, granting the assertion of the Jews that Jesus died on the cross, presented to the Gentiles the crucified Jesus as an atonement and ransom for the sins of the world, a belief similar to what they already believed concerning their own gods.

St. Paul says: 'In [Jesus] whom we have redemption through his blood, *even* the forgiveness of sins'.[3] He also called his blood 'the blood of his cross';[4] in Hebrews, 'the blood of sprinkling'.[5] John says: 'He is the propitiation for our sins: and not for ours only, but also for the *sins of* the whole world'.[6] The various authors commenting on this in their commentary say: 'There was wrath in the bosom of God at sin: but, through the sacrifice of Christ for sin offered once for all, He has "turned away all His wrath," and can be just'.

The prevalent belief among Christians is that Adam sinned by eating of the forbidden fruit, and in his fall all mankind, his descendants, fell and inherited sin from him. There was no other way for redemption from the sin except that God out of His mercy should send His only begotten Son, blameless, sinless, and

---

1. H. Rashdall, *The idea of Atonement*
2. Weigall. *Paganism in our Christianity*, p. 160
3. Colossians 1:14
4. Colossians 1:20
5. Hebrews 12:24
6. 1 John 2:2

innocent, 'very God and very man': who truly suffered, died and was buried to reconcile his Father to us, and to be a sacrifice, not only for original but also for all actual sins of men.[1]

Before I make any remark on this doctrine I should like to make it clear to Christian readers that I have no intention or wish whatsoever to injure the feelings of my fellow beings. The sole object for which I have taken the trouble of compiling this booklet is to put before them, for their consideration the Islamic point of view concerning crucifixion, resurrection and redemption, so that the gulf of differences in our beliefs may be bridged and we become one spiritually as we are one physically. I give below my remarks which show the incomprehensibility of the doctrine of redemption.

1. The Redemption theory is found on the supposition that all the inhabitants of the globe are descendants of Adam and Eve who existed six thousand years ago, or earlier. Modern science has proved that mankind is much older than the biblical Adam and Eve,[2] verses 14–17 of the fourth chapter of Genesis also indicate that there were men living in parts of the earth other than the residence of Adam and Eve, because Cain said, 'I shall be a fugitive and a vagabond in the earth...every one that findeth me shall slay me'. And the Lord set a mark upon Cain, lest any finding him should kill him. Then he left the place where his parents lived and 'dwelt in the land of Nod on the East of

---

1. *The Book of Common Prayer*
2. At least see: *New discoveries to the Antiquity of man,* by Sir Arthur Keith.

Edom. And Cain knew his wife; and she conceived and bore Enoch; and he built a city after the name of his son Enoch.'

Now, if there were no other living men besides the sons of Adam and Eve, why did the Lord put a mark on Cain that he might not be killed by anyone, and from where did he get his wife? And how did he build the city if there were no other citizens besides himself, living in that part of the land?

The fifth chapter of Genesis also indicates that at the time of the creation of man, the Lord created them male and female and blessed them, and called their name Adam in the days when they were created.[1]

It shows that other men were also called 'Adam', and it was a common name given to all created men. When it is established that all men are not the descendants of the Adam who is supposed to have sinned, then the doctrine of Redemption, based on the fall of Adam in sin, crumbles to pieces.

2. In fact, no person can be a sinner deserving punishment until he breaks intentionally and knowingly, and not ignorantly, a commandment of God. In view of this definition of sin, Adam was not a sinner at all. It is apparent from Genesis 2:18 that God informed him that he was going to make 'an help meet' for him. And when he asked for his reason for eating of the forbidden tree he rightly replied: 'The woman whom thou gavest *to be* with me, she gave me of the tree, and I did eat' (Gen 3:12). And when the woman was questioned by God, 'What *is* this *that* thou hast done?' she replied: 'The serpent beguiled

---

1. Gen. 5:2

me and I did eat.' She confessed that she only was beguiled, which shows that she did not tell Adam that it was from the forbidden tree that she had given him. Adam did not therefore commit a real sin. St. Paul has expressed a similar view when he said 'And Adam was not deceived, but the woman being deceived was in the transgression.'[1] The reason for the expulsion from the Garden of Eden given in Genesis is ridiculous. It runs thus: 'And the Lord God said, Behold, the man is become as one of us, to know good and evil: and now, lest he put forth his hand, and take also of the tree of life, and eat, and live for ever: Therefore, the Lord God sent him forth from the garden of Eden.'[2]

Can anyone believe that God created man to keep him in ignorance of good and evil? Did He not create him in His own image and after His likeness?[3] This passage clearly indicates that Adam's expulsion from the garden was due to the fear of God that he might eat of the tree of life and not in that he had sinned. It is, therefore, clear that the doctrine of Redemption, based on the sin of Adam, is also untrue. In the Holy Quran God says:

And verily, We had made a covenant with Adam beforehand, but he forgot; and We found in him no determination *to disobey*.[4]

---

1. 1 Tim. 2:14

2. Gen. 3:22–23

3. Gen. 1:26–27

4. The Holy Quran, 20:116

3. The assertion that all men sin and that nobody can be justified by the law in the sight of God without believing in the ransom paid by Jesus for his Original Sin, is absolutely wrong. We read in Luke, chapter 1, verse 6, that both Zacharias and his wife 'were both righteous before God, walking in all the commandments and ordinances of the Lord blameless'. Mary, the mother of Jesus, according to the belief of Roman Catholics, was sinless.

4. Original Sin is only an invention of the Pagan Christian, and it is nowhere mentioned in the Old Testament. The opinion of the Christian divines is divided on this question.

> In the 5th century, Pelagius declared the capacity of every man to become virtuous by his own efforts, and summoned the members of the Church in Rome to enter on the way of perfection in monasticism. His friend, Caelestius, was in 412 charged with and excommunicated for heresy, because he regarded Adam as well as all his descendants as naturally mortal, denied the racial consequences of Adam's fall, asserted the entire innocence of newborn, recognised sinless men before the coming of Christ. Pelagius insisted that sin was an act not a state, an abuse of the freedom of the will and that each man was responsible and liable to punishment only for his own acts.[1]

And our religion Islam, the religion of reason and wisdom, does not recognise Original Sin. A child is born with a pure

---

1. Ency. Britt. edition 11.

nature and not as St. Paul says (Eph. 2:3): 'We...were by nature the children of wrath'; that is, liable to punishment.

5. The natural sequence of eating or touching the forbidden tree was death: 'lest ye die'.[1] If it were true that Jesus, by his crucifixion, paid the ransom for Original Sin, then no one should have died after it. But we see that the death sentence is still being carried out; all men die, and the Christian nations, especially, have invented the most cruel and swiftest ways of death.

6. The belief that by killing His innocent Son, God reconciled His justice and mercy, is certainly incomprehensible. 'Moral justice cannot take the innocent for the guilty, even if the innocent would offer himself. To suppose that justice does this is to destroy the principles of its existence; which is the thing itself. It is then no longer justice. It is indiscriminate revenge.'[2]

When Judah requested Joseph to take him instead of his younger brothers, Joseph answered: 'God forbid that I should do so: *but* the man in whose hand the cup is found, he shall be my servant; and as for you, get you up in peace unto your father.'[3]

A positive proof that the doctrine of Atonement is false and contrary to divine justice is that, when the Israelites made a god of gold, a calf, Moses said to them (Exodus 32:30):

---

1. Gen. 3:3
2. *The Age of Reason,* by T. Paine.
3. Gen. 44:17

CHAPTER TEN—REDEMPTION OR ATONEMENT

Ye have sinned a great sin: and now I will go up unto the Lord; peradventure I shall make an atonement for your sin.

Then Moses made two proposals to God (Exodus 32:32): 'If thou wilt forgive their sin—; and if not, blot me, I pray thee, out of thy book which thou hast written.'

Here Moses offered himself as an atonement for the sin of his people—which Jesus never did—but God's answer to his entreaty was that it is against His justice to take the innocent for the guilty, saying: 'Whosoever hath sinned against me, him will I blot out of my book' (Exodus 32:33). The killing of an innocent person for a guilty one is, therefore, directly contrary to justice as well as to mercy. Thus God, instead of reconciling His attributes of mercy and justice, destroyed them both.

7. The assertion that Jesus, the righteous, was made the propitiation for the sin of the whole world[1] is not only incomprehensible, but is also contrary to the axiom of the Old Testament: 'The wicked *shall be* a ransom for the righteous and the transgressor for the upright.'[2]

8. The belief that Jesus, after his death on the cross, was in Hell for three days, during which he suffered the penalty of the sins of the world, is directly contrary to what Jesus himself said to

---

1. 1 John 2:2
2. Prov. 21:18

one of the two thieves who were crucified with him: 'Verily I say unto thee, To day shalt thou be with me in paradise.'[1]

9. It seems absurd to believe that Satan, who is said to have deceived Eve in the form of a snake, at last compelled the Almighty to exhibit Himself on the cross in the form of His Son Jesus, instead of his being exhibited himself by Almighty God, in the form of a snake on the cross. Thus, the Christians make the Almighty fall and the deceiver, Satan, triumph.

10. The idea that by believing in the blood of Jesus a man will be saved and redeemed from the punishment of sin, is directly opposed to the following sayings of Jesus:

(a) 'But I say unto you, That every idle word that men shall speak, they shall give account thereof in the day of judgment. For by thy words thou shalt be justified and by thy words thou shalt be condemned.'[2]

(b) In Matt. 12:32 he says: 'And whosoever speaketh a word against the Son of man, it shall be forgiven him: but whosoever speaketh against the Holy Ghost, it shall not be forgiven him, neither in this world, nor in the *world* to come.'

(c) 'Wherefore if thy hand or thy foot offend thee, cut

---

1. Luke 23:43
2. Matt. 12:36–37

them off, and cast them from thee: it is better for thee to enter into life halt and maimed, rather than having two hands or two feet to be cast into everlasting fire.'¹

(d) 'So shall it be at the end of the world: the angels shall come forth, and sever the wicked from among the just, and shall cast them into the furnace of fire: there shall be wailing and gnashing of teeth.'²

(e) Jesus said (Matt. 6:14–15): 'For if ye forgive men their trespasses, your heavenly Father will also forgive you: But if you forgive not men their trespasses, neither will your Father forgive your trespasses.'

(f) If you read the 25th chapter of Matthew, verses 31 to 46, you will learn that the righteous will go into life eternal For their good deeds done in this world, and those who will be on the left hand 'shall go away into everlasting punishment', for not doing good deeds. All these people of the right and the left will be Christians who believed in Christ. These sayings of Jesus cannot be reconciled with the doctrine of Redemption.

11. Thomas Paine writes:

I well remember, when about seven or eight years of age,

---

1. Matt. 18:8
2. Matt. 13:49–50

hearing a sermon read by a relation of mine, who was a great devotee of the Church, upon the subject of what is called Redemption by the death of the Son of God. After the sermon was ended I went into the garden, as I was going down the garden steps, I revolted at the recollection of what I had heard, and thought to myself that it was making God Almighty act like a passionate man that killed his son when he could not avenge himself in any other way: and as I was sure a man would be hanged that did such a thing, I could not see for what purpose they preached such sermons. This was not one of those thoughts that had anything of childish levity; it was to me a serious reflection arising from the idea I had that God was too good to do such an action, and also too Almighty to be under any necessity of doing it. I believe in the same manner to this moment; and I moreover believe that any system of religion that has anything in it that shocks the mind of a child cannot be a true system.[1]

12. A Christian might say here, as Christians usually do: 'If I owe a person money, and cannot pay him, and he threatens to put me in prison, another person can take the debt upon himself and pay it for me. Thus Jesus, the Son of God, had paid the ransom for our sins for having been in Hell for three days and three nights.' It might be justifiable if sin were taken as a debt, and the debtor, unlike God, be so powerless and poor, or mean and revengeful, that being fully aware of one's inability, he does

---

1. Thomas Paine. *The Age of Reason*. p. 41.

not forgive the debt or respite until you are able to repay him. But if sin is taken as a crime, i.e., breaking the commandments of God wilfully, no law of justice would punish anyone but the culprit, or if it is defined as a spiritual disease, it cannot be cured if the remedy is applied to any other, save the sinner. Moreover, Jesus did not offer himself, but supplicated and prayed to God with tears that He might save him from death. And in most appealing words he then said: 'O my Father, if this cup may not pass away from me, except I drink it, thy will be done.'[1]

Then he made a heart-rending cry while he was on the cross: 'My God, my God, why hast thou forsaken me?'[2] And about Judas, who disclosed to the Jews his hiding place, he said: 'Woe unto that man...it had been good for that man if he had not been born.'[3]

Can anyone honestly say that he offered himself willingly for the guilty ones?

The consequence of this fabricated doctrine is that Christian Europe is becoming the source of Atheism and even the sense of sin has died in it. Rev. H. R. Gough writes:

> Large numbers of our people have no sense of sin at all; they may not be actually immoral themselves, but they have no morals. Conscience has become so dulled by continual disobedience to its promptings that there is no longer a sense of right or wrong. We seem to be no longer

---

1. Matt. 26:42
2. Matt. 27:46
3. Matt. 26:24

ashamed of our sins. When a people comes to that point, disaster is at hand.[1]

Why should they be ashamed of their sins? Has not God, out of His mercy, shed the blood of His innocent Son (even of Himself) for their redemption? This doctrine, however, gives a free licence to commit sins and has resulted in the Christians of Europe and America committing crimes of indecency more openly than anywhere else in the world: not only the ordinary Christians but preachers and the priests as well. See: The Crimes of Preachers; published New York: The Crimes of Christianity, by J. M. Wheeler, (London, 1887); Life, by the Nun of Kenmere; Inside the Church of Rome; Life inside the Church of England; and Why is Christianity a Failure? by a Churchman, published by Ideal Publishing Union, Ltd., London.

At all events sin still exists, especially in the Christian world; and I do not think Pauline Christianity can offer Christians any remedy for the forgiveness of their sins. St. Paul says: 'For if we sin wilfully after that we have received the knowledge of the truth, there remaineth no more sacrifice for sins.'[2] The sinful Christian world which commits sins after believing in the Crucified Christ shall die in sin, and according to the aforesaid saying, will never get salvation.

---

1. *The Watchman*, March 1941, p. 93 (London).
2. Hebrews 10:26

The True Atonement

In 1943, the Secretary of the Society of Friends of the Muslims in China, in a letter to me, explained her belief in these words:

> God came in the person of Christ and took the sin (not only the punishment but the sin itself) upon Himself. Without the death of Jesus, sin cannot justly be forgiven and made righteous.

My answer to her was that this belief is tantamount to believing that God committed suicide on the cross and went into Hell for three days, and that He has no right to forgive His creation their sins without punishing them: And that He is not compassionate nor merciful, but like a judge who is bound to punish the culprit according to the law given to him by higher authorities. Is it mercy to kill an innocent person for others? Ask any compassionate father who has an only son, what kind of mercy and justice that would be? To think that sins can be washed out by the blood of Jesus is not only irrational, but also inconsistent with all conceptions of mercy and justice as well.

The conception of God which Islam has presented to the world is that He is Merciful, Compassionate, and Most Forgiving to His servants. God says in the Holy Quran:

> Say, 'O My servants who have acted extravagantly against

their own souls, do not despair of the mercy of Allah; surely He is the Most Forgiving, the Merciful.'[1]

He is the sole Master and Creator of all men. He may forgive whom He likes and may punish when the punishment would benefit the culprit. [Read the parable of the householder who hired men, and who, in the end, said (Matt 20:15): 'Is it not lawful for me to do what I will with mine own?' The master has, therefore, the right to forgive his servants also.]

When a sinner falls down and puts his forehead on the threshold of the Most Compassionate God and repents and prays with a broken heart and streaming eyes, with the determination that he will never commit sin again; then God, who is more compassionate than either mother or father, moved with compassion, comes to his rescue and forgives his sins. This is the way by which sin can justly be forgiven. Have you not read the parable of a certain king who took account of his servant who owed him ten thousand talents? But the servant fell down and worshipped him, saying, 'Lord, have patience with me, and I will pay thee all.' Then the Lord of that servant was moved with compassion, and loosened him, and forgave him the debt.'[a]

---

1. The Holy Quran, 39:54

(a) She answered that she had read it, 'but it must have cost him a good deal of sacrifice. That enormous amount of capital.' I replied, 'Think, if a man can write off a debt despite the enormous cost, then how much more possible will it be for Omnipotent, All-Possessing God to forgive while it does not cost Him anything? The parable shows that repentance and supplication is the true way for obtaining forgiveness. But you believe that God, without shedding the blood of an innocent, or in other words by committing suicide, could not be justified in forgiving sins.'

When Peter the Apostle inquired of Jesus, 'How oft shall my brother sin against me, and I forgive him? till seven times?' Did he not answer, 'Until seventy times seven'?[1] If men out of their compassion and mercy can forgive those who sin against them, without punishment, why will it be unjust if God, the Merciful God, out of His mercy and grace forgives those who sin against Him, without punishment? The true way for forgiveness of sin is repentance, as is mentioned in the Holy Quran and as was taught by all the divine prophets. God says in the Holy Quran, concerning the sinners:

> They will be saved from punishment, those who repent and believe and do good deeds; these are they of whom Allah changes the evil deeds to good ones and Allah is Forgiving and Merciful.[2]

Ezekiel, the Prophet, says that the Lord said to him:

> The soul that sinneth, it shall die. The son shall not bear the iniquity of the father, neither shall the father bear the iniquity of the son: the righteousness of the righteous shall be upon him, and the wickedness of the wicked shall be upon him. But if the wicked will turn from all his sins that he hath committed, and keep all my statutes, and do that which is lawful and right, he shall surely live, he shall not die. All his transgressions that he hath committed,

---

1. Matt. 18:21–22
2. The Holy Quran, 25:70–71

they shall not be mentioned unto him: in his righteousness that he hath done he shall live.[1]

Read also 2 Chronicles, chap. 7, verses 12–14; and Isaiah, chap. 55, verse 7, in which humility, prayer, the seeking of God's face and the forsaking of the way of wickedness and unrighteousness are the means by which sins might be forgiven.

The death of Jesus on the cross, therefore, as Christians believe, is not the means by which sin can be forgiven. It is in itself a great sin to believe that Merciful God shed the blood of an innocent person for the sins of others, and cursed him. I tell you in all sincerity that Jesus, if he were crucified not once but a thousand times, could not by his death redeem the people of their sins. How appropriate it would be for us to escape the punishment of our sins, to accuse God's beloved prophet Jesus of being cursed by the death on the cross, which means that his heart abandoned God and he became disobedient to Him. One of the purposes why God has sent the Promised Messiah in this age, is to exonerate Jesus from the curse of the death on the cross. This is God's will and His will be done. The time is coming when all Christians, gifted with reason and wisdom, will give up all irrational dogmas borrowed from paganism. Jesus was but a prophet of God whom God saved from the accursed death on the cross and caused him to die a natural death like other great divine prophets.

---

1. Ezekiel 18:20–22

CHAPTER ELEVEN—
JESUS GOES TO INDIA

Where did Jesus Go?

Here arises a question, 'If Jesus did not die on the cross nor ascend to heaven, where did he go?'

Those who know nothing about his whereabouts after he bade his disciples the last farewell would say that he must have gone and died somewhere. His case in this respect is like that of a person who is compelled to bid farewell to his countrymen, goes away to an unknown place and never returns to see them again. Consequently, he is taken as dead after the lapse of the usual span of life. Professor Heinrich Eberhard Gottlob Paulus (1761–1851), for instance, who believed that Jesus did not die on the cross writes:

> Where Jesus really died, they (the Disciples) never knew, and so they came to describe his departure as an ascension.[1]

Likewise, Ernest Brougham Docker, District Court Judge, Sydney, says:

> If Jesus did not die upon the cross, how, where and when did he withdraw from this earthly stage? We must admit that we have no evidence to enable us to answer. For myself, I am content to believe that, being man, he passed through the same gate. 'The strait and dreadful passage of death that all others of human kind must go through.' It may be that Jesus never left his Galilean refuge, but suffered a lingering death from his wounds at his lonely camp fire by the Tiberian lake, or on some solitary mountain summit, or in some secluded valley and that 'No man knoweth of his sepulchre until this day'.[2]

Those who, in the light of the facts and reason, deny Jesus' death on the cross, and his soaring to Heaven, believe in his natural death, but cannot say when and where.

In modern times, when thinking people of Europe, due to their inability to trace his burial place began to take the whole story of his life for a myth, a voice arose from the heart of India in the closing years of the last century, from Qadian—an unknown village then, but now a flourishing centre of Islamic revival—proclaiming

---

1. Dr. Schweitzer. *The Quest of the Historical Jesus,* p. 55.
2. Docker: *If Jesus did not Die upon the Cross?* pp. 70 and 78.

that Jesus, who had been wrongly worshipped as God for centuries, and whose abode was believed to be in the third heaven[1], was lying buried in Khanyar Street, Srinagar, Kashmir.

This voice, supported with cogent arguments, convinced hundreds of thousands of reasonable persons, that the occupant of the tomb was Jesus, son of Mary, prophet of the lost sheep of the House of Israel.

This discovery, God willing, is destined to create a revolution in Christendom and to cause hundreds of millions to give up the worship of a human being and other dogmas borrowed from paganism. The discoverer of the tomb of Jesus is the prophet of this age whose appearance was foretold by the prophets of various nations, and in his person the prophecy concerning the second advent of Jesus has been fulfilled.

Muhammad, may peace and blessings of God be upon him, according to the Holy Quran and the prophecy of Moses in Deut. 18:18, was the like of Moses, peace be upon him, and Ahmad, peace be on him, the prophet of this age, is the like of Jesus, peace be upon him, as he was the object of the prophecy of his second advent.

The Sepulchre of Moses

We read in Deut. 34:6 that 'No man knoweth the sepulchre of his [i.e., Moses] unto this day.' Moreover, his end, like that of Jesus, 'remains surrounded with legends'.

---

1. 2 Corinthians, 12:2

Having taken leave of the people, he was going to embrace Eleazar and Joshua on Mount Nebo, when a cloud suddenly stood over him and he disappeared, though he wrote in scripture that he died, which was done from fear that people might say, that because of his extraordinary virtue, he had been turned into a divinity. (Ant. iv:8 and 48.) Later the belief became current that Moses did not die but was taken up to heaven like Elijah.[1]

His burial place remained unknown for nearly two thousand years until 'his like', i.e., the Holy Prophet Muhammad (peace and the blessings of God be upon him) appeared and discovered it. He said: 'When Moses' death drew nigh he asked God that he should be allowed to go to within a stone's throw from the Promised Holy Land, and there he died.' Abu Hurairah, the reporter, says that the Holy Prophet added: 'If I were there I would have shown you his sepulchre, situated near the roadside, at the foot of a russet hued hillock.'[2]

The specified tomb, in Palestine is known to the Muslims as *Qabr Nabi Musa,* i.e., the tomb of Moses the prophet.[3]

---

1. Jewish Ency., 'Moses'.
2. *Sahih-ul-Bukhari,* vol. 2, 191, Egypt 1932.
3. 'The grave of Moses,' writes Dr. Phillip 'is located between the Dead Sea and Mar Saba. It is marked by the Mosque of Neby Musa and is a great resort of Moslem pilgrims at the Easter season. I saw a vast picturesque procession passing through St. Stephen's Gate in Jerusalem to the valley of the Kedron and on the tomb of the prophet Musa.' 'Through Bible Lands,' page 303 footnote, by Dr. Phillip Schabb, London, James Nisbet & Co., New Edition, September 1888.

Likewise Jesus' tomb remained unknown to the world for nearly the same period of two thousand years, and it was only discovered by Ahmad, the Promised Messiah, the like of Jesus, and is now recognised, by hundreds of thousands, as *Qabr Nabi Isa*, i.e., the tomb of Jesus, the prophet. This is the Lord's doing and it is marvellous in our eyes. Hazrat Ahmad, the prophet of this age, has discussed this question in detail in his book *Masih Hindustan Mein* ('Jesus in India'), but, in view of the size of this booklet, I will only mention a few points concerning this discovery.

The Lost Tribes of Israel

The twelve tribes continued united under one head, making but one state and one people, till after the death of Solomon; then ten tribes of Israel revolted against the House of Israel, received for their King, Jeroboam, while only the tribes of Judah and Benjamin continued under the Government of Rehoboam (I Kings 12:16–20). This separation may be looked upon as the chief cause of those calamities that afterwards fell upon those two kingdoms, and on the whole Hebrew nation. Tiglath-Pileser, first carried away captives, the tribes of Reuben, Gad, Naphtali, and half the tribe of Manasseh; that were beyond the Euphrates (II Kings, 15:29; 1 Chron. 5:26). Some years after, Shalmaneser, King of Assyria, took the city of Samaria, destroyed it, took away the rest of the inhabitants of Israel, carried them beyond the Euphrates, and sent other inhabitants into the country to cultivate and possess it (II Kings 17:6, 24, and 18:10–11). This ended the Kingdom of the Ten Tribes of Israel. The greater part of the Fathers and interpreters are of the opinion that those ten exiled tribes never returned to their own country. Others, on the contrary, think that they did return, but at the same time they acknowledge that this return is not clearly made out by history[a] as was not so complete and entire, but that a great number of Israelites still remained beyond the Euphrates.[2]

Alfred Edersheim, writes:

(a) This thought not only has no historical proof, but it seems to be an imaginary one. Had they returned to their mother country they could have been found in a great majority at all times in Palestine which in the light of history, is not the case. A certain professor has supported this imaginary thought with the phrase of the 'twelve tribes' used in the N.T. But a phrase cannot alter historical facts. The various authors in their commentary on the Bible, in their note on Joshua 4:2, say:—

So even when the great majority of the tribes had been lost in the captivity, the Jews, as they claimed for themselves the position and promises given to all Israel of old, fondly spoke of the twelve tribes, as if they still literally existed, though now represented only by themselves.

The view of H. S. Kehimkar (1830–1899) in this regard in his book, *The History of the Beni Israel of India,* p. 6, seems to me more accurate. He says that on the fall of the kingdom of Israel the ten tribes were not driven away entirely, for according to Chron., chap. 30, remnants here and there were still left in Palestine. In like manner 130 years later when the kingdom of Judah fell, remnants of that people were still left in Palestine. In view of those remnants the usage of the term 'twelve tribes' was quite right.

2. *A Complete Concordance to the Holy Scripture,* by Alexander Cruden, M.A. Tribe.

In general it is of the greatest importance to remember in regard to the Eastern dispersion, that only a minority of the Jews, consisting in all of about 50,000, originally returned from Babylon, first under Zerubbabel and afterwards under Ezra (537 B.C. and 459/8 B.C.) Nor was their inferiority confined to members. The wealthiest and the most influential Jews remained behind. According to Josephus (Ant. 11, 5), with whom Philo substantially agrees, vast numbers estimated at millions, inhabited the Trans-Euphratic Provinces. A later tradition has it, that so dense was the Jewish population in the Persian Empire, that Cyrus forbade the further return of the exiles, lest the country should be depopulated. So large and compact a body soon became a political power. 'The Babylonian "dispersion" had already stretched out its hands in every direction eastward it had passed as far as India'. Still the great mass of the ten tribes was in the days of Christ, as in our own, lost to the Hebrew nation.[1]

In the fourth book of Ezra (13:39–45) it is declared that the ten tribes were carried by Hosia, King in the time of Shalmaneser to the Euphrates, to the narrow passages of the river, whence they went on for a journey of a year and a half, to a place called Arzareth.[2] 'Nebuchadnezzar stormed Jerusalem (586 B.C.), plundered and burnt the Temple, ... and carried off the most illustrious

---

1. Alfred Edersheim, *The Life and Times of Jesus the Messiah*, p. 8, 13, 16, London, 1906.
2. Jewish Ency. 'Tribes.'

and wealthy of the inhabitants prisoners to Babylon. The Israelites who had been exiled 134 years before the inhabitants of Judah, never returned. What became of them has always been, and we presume will always remain a matter of vaguest speculation.'[1]

The Israelites in India

It is patently clear from the aforesaid quotations that the ten tribes were lost and scattered in various countries. As my subject concerns only India, let us see, therefore, if we can find any trace of these lost tribes in the regions of India.

Modern investigation has shown that the Afghans, Kashmiris, and the Beni Israel of Bombay are the descendants of Israel.

1. We read in the *Jewish Encyclopaedia,* under *Tribes*:

> Abraham Farissol identifies the river Ganges with the river Goxan and assumes that the Beni Israel of India are the descendants of the Lost Ten Tribes. A Christian traveller, Vincent of Milan, who was a prisoner in the hands of the Turks for twenty-five years, and who went as far as Fez, thence to India, where he found the River Sambation and a number of Jews dressed in silk and purple. They were ruled by seven kings, and upon being asked to pay tribute

---

1. Chambers. Ency., 'Jews.'

to the Sultan Salim, they said they had never paid tribute to any sultan or king.

Afghans.—According to their native traditions, the Afghans also are to be identified with the Lost Ten Tribes. They declare that Nebuchadnezzar banished them into the mountains of Ghor, whence they maintained correspondence with the Arabian Jews: Subsequently they became Muslims (Malcolm, 'History of Persia', 11,596, London, 1815). The Afghans still call themselves 'Beni Israel' and are declared to have a markedly Jewish appearance. Their claim to Israelitish descent is allowed by most Muslim writers. G. Moor, in his *Lost Tribes,* p. 143–160, London, 1886, also identified the Afghans with the Ten Tribes.

2. Sir Henry Yule, K.C.S.I., says:—

The Afghan chroniclers call their people Beni-Israel (Arabic for Children of Israel) and claim descent from King Saul (whom they call by the Mohammedan corruption Talut) through a son whom they ascribe to him, called Jeremiah, who again had a son called Afghanna. The numerous stock of Afghanna were removed by Nebuchadnezzar and found their way to the Mountains of Ghor and Feroza east and north of Hirat.

3. James B. Frazer, in his book *Historical and Descriptive Account of Persia and Afghanistan,* p. 298 (New York, 1843), writes:—

According to their (Afghan) own traditions, they believe

themselves descended from the Jews; and in a history of the Afghans (by Neamat-ullah, translated by the Translation Society) written in the 16th century and lately translated from the Persian, they are derived from Afghan, the son of Jeremiah, the son of Saul, King of Israel, whose posterity being carried away at the time of the Captivity, was settled by the conqueror in the mountains of Ghor, Kabul, Candhar and Ghazni. They preserved the purity of their religion until they embraced Islam.

4. In the *Civil and Military Gazette* (November 23rd, 1898) was published a paper on this subject, in which the writer says: 'They, the Afghans, trace their descent from Israelitish tribes.' After having mentioned that their names are Israelitish and that they keep the Feast of the Passover, the writer says: 'Thus the Afghan may possibly be an Israelite, absorbed into ancient Rajput tribes, and this has always appeared to me to be the most probable solution of the problem of his origin.' Then he says that A. K. Johnston has quoted the following tradition: 'When Nadir Shah arrived at Peshawar, the chiefs of the tribes in the Yusuf Zais presented him with a Bible written in Hebrew, and several articles that had been used in their ancient worship which they had preserved; those articles were at once recognised by the Jews that followed the camp.'

5. H.W. Bellews, writes:—

The traditions of this people (Afghans) refer them to Syria as the country of their residence at the time they were carried away into captivity by Bukhtanasar (Nebuchadnezzar) and planted as colonists in different parts of Persia and Media. From these positions they, at some subsequent period, emigrated eastward into the mountainous country of Ghor, where they were called by the neighbouring people 'Bani Afghan' and 'Bani Israel', i.e., children of Afghan and children of Israel. In corroboration of this we have the testimony of the Prophet Esdras to the effect that the ten tribes of Israel who were carried into captivity, subsequently escaped and found refuge in the country of Arzareth, which is supposed to be identical with the Hazarah country of the present day and of which Ghor forms a part. It is also stated in the *Tabaqati Nasiri* that in the time of the native Shansabi dynasty there was a people called Beni Israel living in that country and that some of them were extensively engaged in trade with the countries around.[1,2]

6. Dr. Alfred Edersheim writes:—

---

1. Bellews: *The Races of Afghanistan,* p. 15. Calcutta, 1880.
2. Surgeon Major H. W. Bellews, who has been on political mission at Kabul, delivered two valuable lectures on the subject in the United Service Institute at Simla in September, 1880, published under the title, *A New Afghan Question, or are the Afghans Israelites?* and *Who are the Afghans?* by Cradock & Co. at the Station Press, Simla, 1810. In these lectures Major Bellews has proved Afghans to be Israelites not by the Afghans traditions only but also by the historical facts derived from the Bible and other books. If a reader wishes further information concerning the Afghans descent from Israel I strongly recommend him to read these lectures.

Modern investigations have pointed to the Nestorians, and latterly with almost convincing evidence (so far as such is possible) to the Afghans, as descended from the lost tribes.[1]

7. Col. Sir Thomas H. Holdich, writing on Afghanistan in the Ency. Brit, eleventh ed. says:

> The women have handsome features of Jewish cast. (The last trait often true also of men.)[2]

8. *Kashmiris.*

'M. Manouchi was a native of Venice and chief physician to the Emperor Orangzeb [sic] for above forty years. As he had access to the records of the Mogul empire, and was allowed to translate whatever he chose into Portuguese, the authenticity of his means of information is unquestionable.' Rev. James Hough, quoting from his memoirs the description of the inhabitants of Kashmir, in his book, 'The History of Christianity in India' (London, 1839), writes:

> In the work from which this Chapter [fourth] is principally composed, the author has made an observation upon the appearance and circumstances of some of the inhabitants of Cashmere, which will be specially interesting to persons who, at different periods, have evinced an anxiety

---

1. Alfred E. Edersheim: *The Life and Times of Jesus the Messiah*, p. 15.
2. Ency. Britt., edition 11 *Afghanistan*.

CHAPTER ELEVEN—JESUS GOES TO INDIA

to discover the long lost ten tribes of Israel. We have seen that he makes mention of a Jew at the court of Akbar; and he further says,—'There is an old tradition, that the Jews who were led captive by Shalmaneser settled at Cashmere, and that the people of that country are the descendants of those Jews. It is certain, though we find no traces in that country of the Jewish religion, the people there being all either Gentiles or Mahomedans, that there are several vestiges of a race descended from the Israelites. The air of the face, and the looks of the present inhabitants, have something of what is peculiar to the Jews, which distinguishes them from all other people. *Moses* is a very common name there; and some ancient monuments, still to be seen, discover them to be a people come out of Israel.[12]

In the footnote on page 291 the Rev. Hough says:

Mr. Forster was so much struck with the general appearance, garb, and manners of the Cashmirians, as to think, without any previous knowledge of the fact, that he had

---

1. Hough: *History of Christianity in India*, vol. 2, p. 281, 288, 2. Cartou: General History of the Mogul Empire, extracted from Memoirs of M. Manouchi, p. 195–196.
2. Before relating the old tradition M. Manouchi describes the Kashmiris in these words: 'The very people who inhabit that delightful country have nothing of the effeminacy and slothfulness of the Indians. They are robust and laborious, exercised in tilling their lands, and very brave in war.'

been suddenly transported among a nation of Jews.—See Forster's Travels.

9. Dr. A. Keith Johnston in his Dictionary of Geography, writes:—

> The natives [of Kashmir] are of a tall, robust frame of body, with manly features, the women full formed and handsome, with aquiline nose and features, resembling the Jewish.[1]

10. Dr. Francois Bernier, in his 'Travels in the Mogul Empire: AD 1656–1668' (translated by Archibald Constable), writes:—

> On entering the kingdom [Kashmir], after crossing the *Pire-penjale* mountains, the inhabitants in the frontier villages struck me as resembling *Jews*. Their countenance and manner, and that indescribable peculiarity which enables a traveller to distinguish the inhabitants of different nations, all seemed to belong to that ancient people. You are not to ascribe what I say to mere fancy, the *Jewish* appearance of these villagers having been remarked by our *Jesuit Father*, and by several other Europeans, long before I visited *Kachemire*.

After mentioning a few points in support of his view, he says:—

> You will see then, that I am not disposed to deny that

---

1. Johnston: Dictionary of Geography. *Kashmir*. London, 1867.

Jews may have taken up their residence in *Kachemire*. The purity of their law, after a lapse of ages, may have been corrupted, until having long degenerated into idolatry, they were induced, like many other pagans, to adopt the creed of *Mahomet*. It is certain that many *Jews* are settled in *Persia*, at *Lar* and *Hyspan* [Isfahan]; and in *Hindoustan*, towards *Goa* and *Cochin*.[1]

In the footnote the translator says:—-

The features of Jewish cast of many of the inhabitants of Kashmir is noticed by many modern travellers. The Moslem historian known as Alberuni, who was born A.D. 973, says in his description of Kashmir, talking of the inhabitants:—'They are particularly anxious about the natural strength of their country, and therefore take always much care to keep a strong hold upon the entrances and roads leading into it. In consequence it is very difficult to have any commerce with them. In former times they used to allow one or two foreigners to enter their country, particularly Jews, but at present they do not allow any Hindu whom they do not know personally to enter, much less other people.' (p. 206, vol. 1, English edition by Dr. Edward C. Sachau. London: Trubner, 1888)

11. Sir Francis Younghusband, who had been Political Agent in

---

1. Bernier: *Travels in the Mogul Empire,* translated by A. Constable (1891), p. 430–431. Oxford University Press, 1914.

Chitral 1893–4; British Commissioner to Tibet from 1902–4; and Resident, Kashmir from 1906–9, writes:

> The visitor with an ordinary standard of beauty, as he passes along the river or the roads and streets, does see a great many more than one or two really beautiful women. He will often see strikingly handsome women, with clear-cut eyebrows, and a general Jewish appearance. (p. 125)
>
> Other interesting Kashmir types of Kashmir Mohammedans are found among the head men of the picturesque little hamlets along the foothills. Here may be seen fine old patriarchal types, just as we picture to ourselves the Israelitish heroes of old. Some, indeed, say, though I must admit without much authority, that these Kashmiris are of the lost tribes of Israel.

After having mentioned the theory of the Founder of the Ahmadiyya Movement, that Jesus did not die on the cross, but had been cut down and had disappeared and had come to Kashmir, where he died and was buried in Srinagar, Sir Francis says:

> When the people are in appearance of such decided Jewish cast it is curious that such a theory should exist, and certainly, as I have said, there are real Biblical types to be seen everywhere in Kashmir, and especially among the upland villages. Here the Israelitish shepherd tending his flock and herds may any day be seen.[1]

---

1. 'Kashmir', described by Sir F. Younghusband, K.C.I.E., p. 125, 129, 130.

These opinions, some of which were expressed centuries ago, clearly show that the Jews from the lost ten tribes did settle in Kashmir. The last two opinions are of two Christians who by coincidence had a similar name, 'Francois', a French traveller and 'Francis' an English high official who served in civil and military services in these regions in India.

The former's opinion was expressed before the discovery of Jesus' tomb in Srinagar and the latter after the discovery, but both are unanimous that the Kashmiris seem to be strikingly of Israelitish stock. Indeed, they are, as Sir Francis and M. Manouchi have mentioned, from among the lost ten tribes of the Israelites.

Besides the similarity of Afghan and Kashmiris to the Jews in their features, physical structure, their dress and in some of their customs, there is another strong and convincing proof that they are of Israelite origin. It is a fact—and the European Settlements such as Canada, Australia, etc., confirm it—that the migrants or settlers name their new homes, cities, and regions after the names of their old towns and patriarchs of their mother country. It is a common habit with every nation. The same love we find has been displayed by those of the lost ten tribes who dwelt in Afghanistan and Kashmir. They, besides their own names, named their tribes, mountain, and rivers after the names of their ancient patriarchs such as Musa Khel (the tribes of Moses), Sulaiman Zai (the tribe of Solomon), Daud Zai (the tribe of David), Yusaf Zai (the tribe of Joseph), Koh-i-Sulaiman (the Mount of Solomon), Takht-i-Sulaiman (the throne of Solomon), and the river Cabul. As a

London, Adam & Charles Black, 1911.

specimen I give below a few names of their towns, which are identical with those of old Syriac towns.

	Afghanistan & Kashmir	Syria	Reference
1	Kabul (Capital of Afghanistan)	Cabul	I Kings 9–13
	Zaida (on the frontier)	Zaidon or Sidan (Mod-Saida)	Judges 18–28
2	Hims (near Ladakh)	Hamath	Numbers 13–21
3	Hazarah	Hazarah	Numbers 11–35
4	Gilgit	Golgotha	Matthew 27–33
5	Tibet	Tibbath	1 Chr. 18–8
	Ladakh	Laadah	1 Chr 4–21
	Leh	Lehi (a District)	Judges 15–9

The existence of these and other Biblical names reveal the fact that the Israelites did live in these regions of India.

There is a legend in *Usool Cafi* (a book of Traditions of the Shiah Sect compiled more than a thousand years ago, P. 334), which says that there lived in Kashmir a king whose forty courtiers were well-versed in the knowledge of the Torah (the Mosaic Law) and they used to read the Gospel, Psalms, and the Scriptures of Abraham. When they heard of the appearance of the Prophet Muhammad, peace and the blessing of God be upon him, they sent an emissary or envoy to investigate and in consequence they accepted Islam.

12. *The Beni Israel of Bombay.*

The Beni Israel of Bombay Presidency are also the descendants of Israel. It is said that they founded their homes in India a long time before Jesus. A comprehensive account of this community is given in a valuable book, 'The History of the Beni Israel', written by Hakem Samuel Kehimkar (1830–1899) published in Tel Aviv (Palestine) in 1937. The author first gives the different accounts of this community by various foreign writers. He writes:—

> (1) The late Dr. Wilson gave a short account to the Bombay Branch of The Royal Asiatic Society on its anniversary meeting held in 1838, and published it in the *Lands of the Bible.* He there shows that the Beni-Israel have been established for many ages in his country and takes the view that they belong to the lost ten tribes of Israel. But in this *Appeal for the Christian Education of the Beni-Israel,* published in the year 1866, he abandoned his former opinion. For he stated in his more recent treatise that the ancestors of the Beni-Israel came from Yemen, or Arabia Felix, in the sixth century of the Christian Era.

(2) Israel Joseph Benjamin II, who has also written an account of the Beni-Israel in his work entitled *Eight Years in Asia and Africa from 1846–1855*, which was published in Hanover in 1859, has almost entirely followed Dr. Wilson. He not only owns that the Beni-Israel are real Jews, but says likewise that they are the lineal descendants of the ten tribes, who in the time of Hosea, the last King of Israel, were carried away by the Assyrians.

Then the author starts with the earlier history of the Beni-Israel, and says that after the fall of the kingdom of Israel, and the fall of the kingdom of Judah remnants of that people were left in Palestine. 'A few of the dispersed Hebrews', according to Dr. Issac M. Wise, 'found their way into Ethiopia, Arabia, India and China. Still the bulk of Hebrews of the two former Kingdoms of Israel and Judah, inhabited the Medo-Persian Empire. ...Among the dispersed Hebrews that found their way into India at this time are to be included, we believe, their ancestors of that part of the Jewish Community now found inhabiting the Malabar Coast, who since the arrival of "White Jews" have been known as "Black Jews"'. After discussing the Jewish customs and feasts, etc., held by the Beni-Israel of Bombay Presidency, the author says:—

> We have stated above our firm conviction that the ancestors of the Beni-Israel came directly from Palestine about 175 years before the Christian Era.
> Now if the ancestors of the Beni-Israel had come to India from Yemen or from any other place 1200 years or thereabouts ago, as suggested, they would previously have

given up the practice of making sacrificial meat offering, as has been done by the Jews of other countries, who have ceased to offer such ever since the destruction of the Second Temple. ... Moreover the Jews who had been led into captivity at the time of the destruction of the First Temple and did not return at the close of the 70 years, had already forsaken the custom. But the fact that the practice has been in vogue among the Beni-Israel in India from time immemorial, goes to prove that the ancestors of the Beni-Israel were actually in Palestine during the time of the existence of the Second Temple, and that they left it some time or other before its destruction.[1]

Thus we find that long before the appearance of Jesus the bulk of the lost tribes of the Israelites were living in the North, North-West, South and South-West of India.

The Mission of Jesus

Jesus was the Messiah of the Israelites, and he proclaimed in clear-cut words (Matt 15:24):

I am not sent but to the lost sheep of the house of Israel.

The term 'lost' can be taken in two ways, literal and metaphorical. It can therefore be applied to the lost tribes metaphorically,

---

1. *History of the Beni-Israel of India,* p. 5, 6, 23, Tel Aviv, 1937.

but literally as well. For centuries, they had been away from the Holy Land. No wonder, Jesus enjoined his disciples to 'Go rather to the lost sheep of the house of Israel' (Matt 10:6). Jesus even foretold that he would go in search of those who were lost from the Israelites and would find them. He says, 'And other sheep I have, which are not of this fold: them also I must bring, and they shall hear my voice' (John 10:16). As, according to his aforesaid statement, he was sent to the Israelites only, these other sheep, not belonging to the Palestinian Jews therefore were from the lost ten tribes dispersed in other countries. A similar conclusion can be drawn from another saying of Jesus (Matt 13:57):

> A prophet is not without honour, save in his own country.

To believe, therefore, that Jesus did not go to another country where he was honoured, is tantamount to believing that he passed away without honour. His saying, that his case, in view of the plot of his enemies to destroy him, would be similar to the case of the prophet Jonah, also reveals that as Jonah was honoured by his people after he had been in the belly of the whale, likewise Jesus would be honoured by the lost sheep of the House of Israel after he had been in the heart of the earth; i.e., hewn chamber serving for a tomb. And so it happened. He went to other countries where the lost sheep lived and was hallowed by them. The story of the wise men from the East who visited Palestine at the birth of Jesus (who evidently were Israelites, because no nation besides them expected the appearance of the Messiah and because of their saying, 'Where is he that is born King of the Jews?') contained a hint that Jesus would be honoured by those sheep who were living in the Eastern countries.

Jesus also mentioned a parable which hinted at the same. He said:

> How think ye? If a man have an hundred sheep, and one of them be gone astray, doth he not leave the ninety and nine, and goeth into the mountains, and seeketh that which is gone astray? And if so be that he find it, verily I say unto you, he rejoiceth more of that *sheep* than of the ninety and nine which went not astray. (Matt 18:12–13)

If it is true what this parable contains, if it is true that Jesus was a good shepherd, if it is true that the ten tribes of Israel were lost and were scattered abroad by foreign powers as divine punishment for their turning away from the right path, and if it is true that he was sent to the lost sheep of the House of Israel, then it was, undoubtedly, his foremost duty to go in search of these lost sheep of the House of Israel and rejoice after finding them.

Jesus, as we believe, a true prophet and beloved of God, could not neglect the duty imposed upon him by God. When he saw that the Palestinian Jews were not going to accept him, and had left no stone unturned to destroy him, he left the country and went in search of the lost sheep, who were not of the fold of the Palestinian Jews.

St. Thomas in India

Before I proceed to trace the footsteps of Jesus, after he left Palestine, I would like to say a few words about the adventures of St. Thomas, one of the twelve disciples of Jesus, who either accompanied his master on his long journey or followed him to fulfil his duty of preaching to the lost sheep of the House of Israel, living in the Far East and India. It should be remembered that it was St. Thomas who, by seeing the print of the nails in Jesus' hands and his wounded side, provided a positive proof that the person seen was not a phantom but Jesus himself with his wounded physical body; and thus he became a witness for all time that Jesus did not die an 'accursed' death. It is a well-established fact that St. Thomas proceeded to India and died there.

1. Dr. Francis C. Burkitt, Professor of Divinity at the University of Cambridge, says:

> Eusebius (H.E. Ill, 1, 1) says, Thomas was the evangelist of 'Parthia' probably because Edessa (q.v.), where some of his bones were preserved is sometimes called 'Edessa of Parthians'. These bones were reputed to have been brought to Edessa from India and a work known as the *Acts of Thomas* relates his missionary labours and martyrdom there ... the *Acts of Thomas* is the leading authority for the earliest Christianity in the countries east of the Eupharates. ...A curious feature is that the name of the

Apostle is given as Judah Thomas, and is expressly set forth that he was the twin of Jesus Christ.⁽ᵃ⁾

It is claimed that the Acts is historical, and further that the scene of the Acts is laid in southern India. Unfortunately for his view, the details in Acts which point to any acquaintance with India at all, are connected with the North West⁽ᵇ⁾ and the country between India and Mesopotamia. 'Christians of St. Thomas' is a name often applied to the ancient Christian churches of southern India; the view taken of their story is so intimately connected with the historicity of 'The Acts of Thomas' that it is convenient to treat of them here.

> According to their tradition, St. Thomas went from Malabar [South-West Coast] to Mylapur, now a suburb of Madras, where the shrine of his martyrdom, rebuilt by the Portuguese in 1547, still stands on Mt. St. Thomas, and where a miraculous cross is shown with a Pahlavi inscription which may be as old as the 7th century. We know from Cosmos Indicopleustes that there were Christian churches of Persian (East Syrian) origin, and doubtless of

---

(a) His being called the twin of Jesus probably means that he from among all his disciples accompanied him in his long journey to India, and preached his message as Jesus' mission was his own mission, otherwise there is no cogent reason for his being called 'twin of Jesus.'

(b) This corroborates our theory. North-West was the place where masses of the lost ten tribes were domiciled. Jesus and his disciple St. Thomas at first came to the North West and then Thomas was sent by Jesus, if he accompanied him: or of his own accord if he followed Jesus, to the South-West of India, where also the Israelites lived.

Nestorian creed, in Ceylon, in Malabar, and at Caliana (north of Bombay) before the middle of the 6th century, and even then St. Thomas, the reputed apostle of Persia, may have been their special saint.[1]

2. Rev. Yeats Brown, after visiting Travancore state, wrote:

> The oldest Christian site, not only in Travancore, but perhaps in the world, is the Syro-Malankaran, whose adherents claim that St. Thomas himself baptised the first of them, when he landed on this coast in 59 A.D. He called them Nazarenes, for the term Christians had not yet come into use. (Acts of the Apostles 11: 26)[2]

3. Archbishop Lord Lang (former Archbishop of Canterbury), in a broadcast speech, said:

> The tradition that St. Thomas went to India has never been disproved, and without doubt Christianity in India has ancient roots.[3]

H. G. Rawlinson C.I.E. writes in his book 'India, A Short Cultural History' (p. 92 to 93):

> One of the Indo-Parthian or Saka princes of Taxila, known

---

1. Ency. Britt. edition 14: 'St. Thomas.'
2. The Spectator, No. 5636, p. 1124, London.
3. Great Britain and the East, Dec. 3, 1936. London.

to Greeks as Gondopharnes, is of especial interest to us because, according to the apocryphal Acts of Thomas, the Apostle Thomas came to his court to preach Christianity. There was formerly a great deal of doubt whether Saint Thomas ever visited India, but recent researches tend to prove that the legend is founded on historical fact, Bartholomew and Thomas were sent to preach the gospel in the East. Thomas probably reached Taxila by the well known sea-route, from Alexandria to the mouth of the Indus. He was hospitably received at the court of Gondopharnes, for Taxila was a cosmopolitan centre of culture and accustomed to give a ready hearing to teachers from strange countries. His missionary labours were, however, interrupted by the Lushan invasion, and Thomas was compelled to flee. He retraced his steps to the mouth of the Indus, and thence took a boat to Muziris, the Roman colony on Malabar coast, touching at Socotra on the way. Here he arrived in A.D. 52 and founded the Church in Malabar. Twenty years later he transferred his labours to the East Coast, and was martyred by the Brahmins. His relics repose in the Cathedral dedicated to him at Mylapore near Madras.* Gondopharnes is a corruption of the Persian Vindaphorna, Bringer of Victory. In the Armenian version of the story, this becomes Gathaspar, from which is derived Gaspar, the name given to the

---

* J.N.Farquhar, *The Apostle Thomas in Southern India,* John Rylands Library Bulletin, 1927, p. 20.

second of the Magi who visited the cradle of the infant Jesus, (p. 92, 93).

L. W. Brown, Bishop of Uganda writes:

> There is evidence that in the Acts 'India' refers to our India, or rather to the area of the North-West Frontier Province now contained in Pakistan. King Gundaphouls and his brother Gad are now known to be historical figures, ruling over the Scytho-India empire east and west of the Indus from about A.D. 19–45.[2] There was a considerable Jewish colony in North-Western India in the first century, which might have attracted the attention of the first Christian missionaries.[3] There are other facts which seem to indicate a northern locus for St. Thomas' work. Bardaisan in his Book of Fate (A.D. 196) speaks of Parthian Christians living among pagans which might be a result of the destruction of the Indian Parthian empire by Kushan invaders about (A.D. 50).[4] There are also said to be Christian tribes still living in north India, but holding their faith a secret from all others. For example, at Indus there is a fakir community which calls itself by an Aramaic name, something like, 'Bartolmai' and claims to have been descended from St. Thomas' converts and to have books and relics to prove it. Unfortunately no outsider has ever been allowed to see this alleged proof.[5][a]

(a) Extract of page No. 47 of the 'Indian Christians of St. Thomas, an account of the ancient Syrian Church of Malabar p. 47, by L.W.Brown,

[*Footnotes cited in the above quote:*]

2. W. R. Philipps, Indian Antiquary, xxxiii, pp. 10ff., 'Trans. of Notes on the Indo-Scythians by Sylvain Levi'; *Camb. Hist. India,* 1, pp. 563–78; Arch. Survey of India, *Annual Report* of 1902–3, p. 167. Some scholars, however, do not now regard the date of Gundaphorus as firmly established.

3. The Kharosttic (Sanskrit in a Semitic script) inscriptions on coins and an Aramaic inscription of one of Asoka's edicts found at Taxila establish this fact; *Journal of Asiatic Studies* (1915) p. 340–7 Herzfeld, *Egripraphia Indica,* xix, p. 251–3 see also N. A. Faris, *The Arab Heritage.*

4. *Camb. Hist. India,* pp. 580–5.

5. R. A. Trotter. 'The History of Christianity in Sind', *Conference,* February, 1947.

Christians and Christianity in India and Pakistan by P. Thomas George Allen, Unwin Ltd., London 1954.

It is quite probable that the Apostle travelled by the overland route to the domains of Gundaphoros and preached the Gospel in his kingdom before South India claimed him. It may be mentioned in this connection that Partha was also associated with the Apostle's activities. There were in Persia and Afghanistan, at the time under the Parthians, a considerable number of Jews of the Dispersion and the anxiety of the Apostle to communicate to his

Bishop of Uganda, formerly Principal Kerela United Theological Seminary Trivandrum. Travencore sometimes Chaplain Fesus and Dowing College Cambridge, Cambridge at the University Press... 1956.'

countrymen the Glad Tidings of the advent of the Messiah must have led him to these regions first. To this day many tribesmen of the Indo-Afghan border claim their descent from Israel.

After preaching the Gospel in Gundaphoros' kingdom, other countries claimed the Apostle's attention. A zealot of Thomas's energy could not find peace as long as a single country remained ignorant of the life and teachings of the Master. The anarchical condition then prevailing in Hindustan proper and news of the existence of numerous Jewish communities on the ports of the West Coast must have influenced the Apostle's decision to proceed to the Malabar Coast from the Kingdom of Gundaphoros.

Thus St. Thomas, by travelling to the regions in which the lost ten tribes lived, fulfilled the duty imposed upon the Disciples by Jesus saying: 'Go rather to the lost sheep of the House of Israel'.

And St. James obeyed this order by writing an Epistle addressing the twelve tribes wherever they might be. He commenced his Epistle with these words: 'James, a servant of God and of the Lord Jesus Christ, to the twelve tribes which are scattered abroad, greeting'.

Jesus in Search of the Other Sheep

The fourth Gospel reveals the fact that Jesus met his disciples for the last time at the Sea of Tiberias, dined with them, told Peter to 'feed my sheep,' bade them his last farewell, and departed for good. Where did he go? The Gospel contains no answer. In the Acts and the Epistles of St. Paul, however, we read that he was seen by St. Paul near Damascus in a vision, but 1 Corinthians 15:8

has led some thinkers to conclude that at the time of the conversion of St. Paul to Christianity, which was between six to twelve months after the crucifixion, Jesus was still in the regions of Syria. Judge Docker, District Court Judge, Sydney, gives the following explanation of the story of Saul's conversion:—

> Jesus, finding he could no longer remain with safety in Galilee, started on his journey to visit the lost tribes of Israel in the East, via Damascus, where he remained a considerable time, long enough to make disciples of Ananias and others. This may have been the reason why the commission was sent by the Jewish authorities to carry out persecutions there. Jesus, knowing of his approach, went out like Elijah of old, to meet his enemy Saul, the result of his wonderful personal power being the conversion of the persecutor into a disciple. The intercourse between them probably continued some days in the house of Ananias, or wherever Jesus was residing. The arrival of the Commission, however, showed Jesus that it was no longer safe for him to remain in Damascus, and he proceeded towards Babylon on his way to the East.

This explanation is supported by Johannes Weiss (*Paul and Jesus*, p. 81):

> Paul's vision and conversion are psychologically inconceivable except upon the supposition that he had been

actually and vividly impressed by the human personality of Jesus.[1]

Jesus in Nisibus[a]

In his book *Masih Hindustan Mein*, the Promised Messiah[as], leaving out the exaggerated accounts, gives the following account from *Rauzat-us-Safa* (p. 130–5), a well-known book of history:

> Jesus (on whom be peace) was named the 'Messiah' because he was a great traveller. He wore a woollen scarf on his head, and a woollen cloak on his body. He had a stick in his hand: wandered from country to country and from city to city. At nightfall he would stay where he happened to be. He ate jungle vegetation, drank jungle water and went on his travels on foot. Journeying from his country he arrived at Nasibin, hundreds of miles from his home. With him were a few of his disciples whom he sent to the city to preach. In the city, however, there were current wrong and unfounded rumours about Jesus (on whom be peace) and his mother. The governor of the city, therefore, arrested the disciples and then summoned Jesus. Jesus

---

1. Docker: *If Jesus did not Die upon the Cross?* p. 75–76.
(a) 'Nisbis (Nasibina in the Assyrian description), modern Nezib or Nasibin is an ancient city and fortress in the Northe of Mesopotamia, near the point where the Mygdonians (modern Jaghjagha) leaves the mountain by a narrow defile. It consists of some 4000 inhabitants, largely Jews.' (Ency. Britt. edition 11).

miraculously healed some persons and performed other miracles. The king of the territory of Nasibin therefore, with all his armies and his people believed him.[b]

This brief statement of *Rauzat-us-Safa*, says the Promised Messiah (peace be upon him) leads to the conclusion that Jesus (peace be upon him) in the course of his travels had arrived at Nasibin, a city between Mosul and Syria. If one travels from Syria toward Persia one would pass through it. Nasibin is 450 miles from Jerusalem and 150 miles from frontier of Persia. The eastern frontier of Persia touches the town of Herat (Afghanistan). In other words, Herat lies on the eastern boundary of Persia. From Herat up to the Khaiber Pass the distance, is nearly 500 miles.

The aforesaid report of *Rauzat-us-Safa* is certainly correct insofar as, after his rejection and persecution by Israel in Palestine, Jesus migrated from Palestine and reached Nasibin; it was in accord with his mission. Josephus, the well-known historian of that time, tells us that Nasibin at that time, was inhabited by the Jews of the lost ten tribes. He says:

> A dreadful calamity now befell the Jews that were in Mesopotamia and especially those that dwelt in Babylonia. There was also the city Nisibis, situated on the same current of the river. (p. 314)
>
> Now the whole nation of the Jews in fear both of the Babylonians and of the Seleucians because all the Syrians

---

(b) The author has mentioned these facts under the caption, 'Flight of Jesus from Jerusalem and manifestation of some miracles on the journey.'

that lived in those places agreed with the Seleucians to war against the Jews: so most of them gathered together, and went to Naarda and Nisibis, and obtained security there from the strength of those cities, and also their inhabitants, who were a great many, and were all war-like men.[1]

From Nasibin Jesus proceeded through Persia into Afghanistan, from whence through Punjab, he entered Kashmir. It appears from legends that he visited Tibet and other regions of India as well, but it seems certain that he lived and, at last, died in Kashmir.

One of the many reasons for Jesus[as] being called the *Masih*, writes the Promised Messiah[as], is that he was a great traveller. A Muslim saint, Abu Bakr Muhammed Attartushi, in his book *Siraj-ul-Malook* (p. 6, Egypt, 1306), calls Jesus 'The Chief of Travellers'.

Likewise in *Lisan-ul-Arab*, an authentic Arabic Lexicon, we read: 'Jesus was named the *Masih* because he wandered about and did not stay in one place.'

In *Kanz-ul-Ummal*, a voluminous collection of the sayings of the Holy Prophet[saw] of Islam and his companions[ra], we read that Abu Hurairah (God be pleased with him) said that God revealed to Jesus[as] the following: 'O Jesus, move from one place to another lest thou shouldst be recognised and persecuted.'

In the same book we read a report from Jabir[ra] that Jesus[as] was constantly on the move. He went from one country to another, and at nightfall, wherever he was, he would eat the vegetation of the jungle and drink pure water.

---

1. *The Works of Flavius Josephus,* Whitson's Translation, with notes, by Sir C. W. Wilson, Vol. 3, p. 324, London, 1889.

Again, in the same book, we find a report from Abdullah[ra] son of Umar[ra] which runs as follows:

> The Holy Prophet (peace and the blessings of God be upon him) declared that the most favoured in the sight of Allah are the *'Gharib'*. Asked what was meant by *Gharib*, he answered: People like Jesus the Messiah who flee from their country with their faith. (vol. 2, p. 34, 71, and vol. 6, p. 51)

These reports about Jesus[as] are not only ancient, but are found in the reliable books of Muslim Tradition. If Jesus[as] remained in Palestine all his life, then he cannot justifiably be called 'The Chief of Travellers'. In view of these reports therefore, which have come to us from various independent sources, we have no option but to believe that Jesus[as] did flee from Palestine and wandered from country to country and, at last, reached India. Thus, he deserved the title 'The Chief of Travellers'!

CHAPTER TWELVE—
THE UNKNOWN LIFE OF JESUS

Buddhists and Jesus

Another proof that Jesus[as] did go to India is the ancient Buddhist writings in which it is explicitly mentioned that Jesus[as] proceeded to India and preached the word of God here and there. John Pinkerton in his book of travels, published in 1811, says:

> Several missionaries have imagined, that in the ancient books of the Lamas, some traces remain of the Christian religion; which as they think, was preached there in the time of the Apostles.[1]

---

1. Pinkerton: *A General Collection of the Best and Most Interesting Voyages and Travels in All Parts of the World,* Vol. 7, p. 554, London 1811.

After the close of the Turko-Russian War (1877–1878) a Russian traveller named Nicholas Notovitch, after visiting many countries, finally (in 1887) reached India. In the course of one of his visits to a Buddhist convent, he learned from the chief Lama that there existed very ancient memoirs, treating the life of Jesus and of the nation of the Occident, in the archives of Lassa. On his return to Europe he arranged the notes containing the life of Jesus. With a view to their publication he submitted them for revision to Monsegneur Platon, the celebrated Archbishop of Kiev. He, though believing the importance of the discovery tried to dissuade him from giving the memoirs publicity, declaring that it would be against his own interest to do so. Why? He refused to explain. A year later he chanced to be in Rome and submitted the manuscript to a cardinal, standing high in the estimation of the Holy Father. 'Why should you print this?' He said: 'Nobody will attach much importance to it, and you will create numberless enemies thereby; and if you need money I can give some compensation for the notes.' This offer he naturally refused. In parts he laid his project before Cardinal Rotelli, whom he had met in Constantinople. He also opposed the publication of the work, under the pretext that it would be premature. 'The Church', he added, 'suffers too deeply from this new current of atheistic ideas: and you would only furnish new food to the detractors of the Evangelical Doctrine.' At last he published his book under title 'The Unknown Life of Jesus'[1], adding:

---

1. In the British Museum I have seen two English translations of this book, which originally was published in French. One of them is by Alexina Loranger, published by Rand McNally & Co., publishers, Chicago and New York, 1894.

Before criticising my work, scientific societies can without much expense, organise an expedition whose mission it would be to study these manuscripts in the locality in which they are to be found, and thus verify their historical value.[1]

The author writes in this book:

> In a recent visit to one of your Gnopas, a lama spoke to me of a Prophet, or as you perhaps call him, a Buddha, of the name of Issa. 'Can you tell me anything of him?' I asked. 'The name of Issa is greatly respected among the Buddhists was the reply, though little is known of him save by the Chief Lamas, who have read the parchments relating to his life.' (p. 90)
>
> Our Gnopa, being among the fortunate ones already possesses a large number of manuscripts, which I read in my leisure hours. Among these copies I have found description of the life and deeds of Issa, who preached in India and among the sons of Israel. (p. 91)
>
> 'In what tongue are written the principal rolls relative to the life of Issa?' I asked.
>
> 'The rolls which treat the life of Issa, and which were brought from India to Nepal, and from Nepal to Tibet,

---

The other is by Violet Crisp, London, Hutchinson & Co.
My references are taken from the first translation.

1. Loranger Translation: *The Unknown Life of Jesus,* pages 8, 9, 12, New York, 1895.

are written in the Pali tongue, and are now at Lassa; but we possess one copy in our own tongue; that is in the Tibetan language.' (p. 93)

Finally yielding to my earnest solicitations, he brought forth two big volumes in cardboard covers with leaves yellowed by the lapse of time, and read the biography of Issa, which I carefully copied from the translation of my interpreter. This curious document is written in the form of isolated verses which frequently bear no connection with each other. (p. 96)

According to these ancient writings, Issa (Jesus) was thirteen years of age when an Israelite should take a wife, he left his father's house, went out of Jerusalem, and in company with some merchants, travelled towards Sind that he might perfect himself in the divine word and study the laws of the Great Buddha. (p. 107)

In the course of his fourteenth year, young Issa (blessed by God) journeyed beyond Sind and settled among Aryas. The fame of his name spread along the Northern Sind. When he passed through the country of the five rivers and Radjipoutada, the worshippers of the god Djaine begged him to remain in their midst. (p. 107)

Then he visited Juggernaut, in the province of Orsis. The white priests of Brahma taught him to read and understand the Vedas, to heal by prayer, to teach and explain the Holy Scripture, to cast out evil spirits from the body of man, and give back to him human semblance. He spent six years in Juggernaut, Rajegriha, Benares, and other holy cities. All loved him for Issa lived in peace with Vaisyas and the Soudras to whom he taught the Holy Scriptures. But the Brahmans and the Kashatriyas opposed him. (p. 108)

I mention below some of the teachings contained in these ancient writings, which Jesus preached to the people in India.

1. God the Father establishes no difference between His children, who are all equally dear to Him. (p. 109)

2. Fear thy God, bow down thy knee before Him only, and to Him only must thy offerings be made.

3. Issa denied the Trimourti and the incarnation of Para-Brahma in Vishnou, Siva and other gods, saying: 'The Eternal Judge, the Eternal Spirit, composes the one and Indivisible soul of the universe, which alone creates, contains and animates the whole' He alone has willed and created. He alone has existed from eternity and will exist without end. He has no equal neither in the heaven nor on this earth. The Great Creator shares His power with no one, still less with inanimate objects as you have been taught, for He alone possesses supreme power. (p. 110)

He willed it, and the world appeared. And He has subordinated to man the land, the waters, the animals and all that He has created and which He maintains in immutable order by fixing the duration of each. The wrath of God shall soon be let loose on man, for he has forgotten his Creator and filled His temples with abomination, and he adores a host of creatures which God has subordinated to him. (p. 111)

The white priest and the warriors becoming cognizant of the discourse, addressed by Issa to the Soudras, resolved upon his death, sent their servants for the purpose in search of the young prophet. (p. 112)

But Issa, warned of this danger by the Soudras, fled in the night from Juggernaut, to the birthplace of the Great Buddha. Six years later, he left Nepal and the Himalayan mountains, descended in the valley of Rajpoutana and went westward, preaching to diverse people of the Supreme Perfection of man. (p. 113)

The fame of Issa's sermons spread to the neighbouring countries, and when he reached Persia, the priests were terrified and forbade the inhabitants to listen to him. (p. 119)

When Issa reached Palestine, he went from place to place strengthening by the word of God the courage of the Israelites, who were ready to succumb under the weight of their despair, and thousands followed him to hear his preaching. (p. 126)

But the rulers of the cities feared him and sent reports against him to Pilate, the Governor of Jerusalem, who ordered that the preacher Issa be arrested and brought before the Judges. He commanded the priests and the learned men, old men of Hebrew origin, to judge him in the temple. (p. 127)

The latter, after hearing Issa, reported to the Governor: 'We have seen the man whom thou accuseth of inciting our people to rebellion, we have heard his preaching and know that he is of our people.' (p. 131)

The Governor sent his spies and at last Issa was arrested and Pilate called together the chief rulers, priests, elders, and law-givers with the object of making them pass judgment on Issa. Then Issa was brought from the prison and he was seated before the Governor between two thieves that were to be tried with him. (p. 140)

But they said to Pilate: 'We will not take upon our heads the great sin of condemning an innocent man and of acquitting two thieves, a thing contrary to our laws. 'Do therefore as thou pleasest.' Having thus spoken the priests and wise men went out and washed their hands in a sacred vessel, saying: 'We are innocent of the death of a just man.' (p. 143) Then by order of the Governor Jesus was nailed to the cross and the two thieves as well. All that day he remained on the cross and in the evening he died. Three days later the Governor sent his soldiers to take up the body of Issa and bury it elsewhere, fearing a general uprising of the people. The following day the sepulchre was found open and empty by the multitude and the rumour immediately spread that the Supreme Judge had sent his angels to take away the mortal remains of the saint. (p. 145)

F. A. Plattner writes in his book *Christian India*:

> In Leh, we again encountered the legend of Christ's visit to these parts. The Hindu postmaster of Leh, and several Ladaki Buddhists told us that in Leh not far from the Bazar, there still exists a pond, near which stood an old tree. Under this tree, Christ preached to the people, before his departure to Palestine. We also heard another legend of how Christ, when young, arrived in India with a merchant's caravan and how he continued to study the higher wisdom in the Himalayas. We heard several versions of this legend which has spread widely throughout Ladakh, Sinkian and Mongolia, but all versions agree on one point that during the time of His absence, Christ was in India and Asia. It does not matter how and from where the legend originated. Perhaps it is of Nestorian origin. It is valuable to see that the legend is told in full sincerity. (p. 29)

According to these scrolls, Issa was 29 years old when he arrived in the land of Israel. This account reveals that the Jews of Palestine did not oppose Jesus but welcomed him, listened to him and stood by him; and it was Pilate, the Roman Governor, who, against their will, unjustly crucified him. Evidently this account directly contradicts the account given by the four Gospel writers.

If we examine it as we do in similar cases of historical events, we would face no difficulty in discovering the truth. It is obvious that the account concerning the crucifixion is not an account of an eyewitness, nor is it by one of the disciples of Jesus. It is only hearsay. It is very probable that the facts were either confused by the original writers, or that the story-teller gave wrong information based on the rumours he had heard.

The author of the book himself writes in this connection:

> It is necessary to remark here that during this period of antiquity, as in our own days, oriental public life was concentrated in the bazaars, where the events of the day and the news from foreign nations were usually followed by a number of dervishes who readily told all they had seen and heard on their journey, in exchange for food. In fact, this was their sole means of subsistence. (p. 150)
>
> The two manuscripts read to me by the lama of Himis Convent, were compiled from diverse copies written in the Tibetan tongue, translated from rolls belonging to Lassa Library and brought from India. Nepal and Maghada two hundred years after Christ. The information contained about Christ is oddly mixed, without relation or coherence with other events of that period. (p. 151)

In view of the Buddhist priests' custom of collecting their information, we cannot take their writings too seriously. In the case of the crucifixion we know nothing about the story-teller or even who he was. Was he a reliable or unreliable person? On the other hand we read in the Gospels a prophecy of Jesus concerning the future of the Jews in which he said that in view of their opposition to him they would be deprived of the Kingdom of Heaven: that is to say, no prophet would appear from amongst them in the future, and this has been literally fulfilled. I have no hesitation, therefore, in saying that the accounts of the Buddhist scrolls cannot be taken as genuine and entirely authentic in view of the account of the Gospels. The only positive conclusion we can draw from these ancient writings is that Jesus did go to India and lived a long time during which he preached the words of God to the people of India. The teachings ascribed to him, some of which I have mentioned above, are truly sublime and worthy of a prophet.

Had Jesus not gone to India there would have been no need for the Buddhist chroniclers to make mention of his preaching in India. On the one hand they could not deny his preaching there and, on the other hand, they found his teachings superior to the teachings of the Buddhists and the Brahmans. Therefore, in order to show the greatness of Gautama Buddha, they purposely confused the events and instead of revealing the fact that Jesus came to India while he was a prophet, and ascribing to him these teachings originally, they ascribed them to Buddha, saying that Jesus came to India in his early age to avoid marriage and to study the law of the great Buddha. Now it is a fact that Buddhism was hardly heard of in Palestine at the time of Jesus. And 'The love of home is so deeply rooted in the human breast that none could even think of severing all ties of kith and kin, unless compelled by dire necessity to do so.' This kind of necessity never existed in the whole life of Jesus except after his narrow escape from the death on the cross, when his very life in Palestine was under constant danger of being destroyed.

There is another point, which I consider advisable to discuss here. The life and the teachings of Buddha bear so close and striking a resemblance to the life and the teachings of Jesus that many thinkers have declared that Christianity is only a copy of Buddhism.

Dr. K. S. MacDonald writes:

Mr. R. C. Dutt begins his chapter on Buddhism and Christianity in his *Ancient India* with the words 'The moral precepts and teachings of Buddhism have so much in common with those of Christianity, that some connection between the two systems of religion has long been suspected.'[1]

Dr. Ernest J. Eitel writes:

Attentive readers will have noticed in this rough sketch of Buddha's life many details singularly coinciding with incidents in the life of our Saviour as reported by the Gospels.

Sakyamuni Buddha, we are told, came from heaven, was born of virgin, welcomed by angels, received by an old saint who was endowed with prophetic vision, presented in a temple, baptised with water and afterwards baptised with fire; he astonished the most learned doctors by his understanding and answers, was led by the spirit into the wilderness and, having been tempted by the devil, the

---

1. Macdonald: *The Story of Barlaam and Joseph;* Introduction, p. xivii. Calcutta, 1895.

friend of publicans and sinners, transfigured on a mount, he descends into hell, ascends to heaven: in short with the single exception of Christ's crucifixion, almost every characteristic incident in Christ's life is also to be found narrated in the Buddhist traditions of the life of Sakyamuni Gautama Buddha. And yet, this Buddha lived and died 275 or even 543 years before Christ. As certain sceptics would make us believe, Christ went to India, during the eighteen years which intervened between his youth and manhood, and returned, thirty years old, to ape and reproduce the life and doings of Sakyamuni Buddha. Or are we to believe in Christ's originality, driven to the miserable subterfuge of assuming as some Jesuit fathers do, that the devil, foreknowing the several details of the Promised Messiah's life, anticipated him and all the details of his life, by his own caricature in Sakyamuni Buddha?[1]

Were the events then of Jesus' life and his teachings truly borrowed from Buddhism, or was it coincidence as Dr. Eital says? Or did he go to India when he was young; or was it a work of the devil, as a certain Jesuit father says? Here is the true answer to this complicated question. Ahmad, the prophet of this age, writes in this connection in his work 'Jesus in India' [*Masih Hindustan Mein*]:

> Now it is worthwhile pondering over the question: Why were there so many resemblances between Buddha and

---

1. Eitel: *Lectures on Buddhism,* Third edition London, 1884.

Jesus? The Aryas, in this respect, say that Jesus became acquainted with Buddhism in the course of his journeys in India, and having acquired knowledge of the facts of the Buddha's life, made his Gospels out of it on his return to his native country. This, however, is a dishonest error of the Aryas. It is quite untrue that Jesus came to India before the event of the cross: he had no need to take such a journey at that time, he had, however, need of taking it when the Jews of *Sham* (Syria) had rejected him and, as they believe, crucified him. Having thus exhausted his sympathy for the Jews and his solicitude to preach to them and, the Jews having become, by reason of their evil nature, so hard-hearted as to be quite incapable of accepting the truth, Jesus, on being informed by God that the ten tribes of the Jews had migrated towards India, set out for those regions. And, as parties of Jews had accepted Buddhism, there was no alternative for this true prophet but to turn his attention to the followers of Buddhism. The Buddhist parties expected the appearance of the Messiah 'Buddha'. Therefore Jesus' titles as well as some of his moral teaching (such as: Love thy enemy; resist evil) and as had been prophesied by Gautama Buddha, concerning the white-coloured *Matiyya* (i.e., *Masiha* or Messiah), for all these signs the priests held him to be the Buddha. It is also possible that some of his titles, moral teachings and the facts of Jesus' life might consciously or unconsciously have been in that age ascribed to Buddha, for the Hindus have never given proof of much experience at recording history. The events of Buddha's life had not been recorded until the time of Jesus.[a]

The Buddhist priests, therefore, had a great opportunity to ascribe to Buddha, anything they wished to ascribe. After relating some examples of the moral teaching, the Promised Messiah[as] writes:—

> Let it be considered, that these moral teachings and this mode of preaching, i.e., speaking in parables (which was the method of Jesus), combined with other circumstances at once suggests that this was imitation of the teaching of Jesus. When Jesus was in India and preached here and there, then the followers of Buddhism met him, and finding him a holy person and man of blessings, recorded these events in their books—Nay, they declared him to be the Buddha, for it is human nature to try and hold a good thing wherever found; so much so, that people try to note and remember any clever remark made by any person before them.

(a) Dr. Eitel writes: 'It can be proved that almost every single tint of this Christian colouring which Buddhist tradition gives to the life of Buddha is comparatively of modern origin. There is not a single Buddhist M.S. in existence which could vie. in antiquity and undoubted authenticity, with oldest codices of the Gospels.' (Eitel: *Lectures on Buddhism,* 3rd ed., London, 1884, p. 16)

Dr. Hermann Oldenberg writes: 'It must be premised as a cardinal statement: a biography of Buddha has not come down to us from ancient times, from the age of Pali texts, and we can safely say no such biography was in existence then.' (Oldenberg: *Buddha, His Life, His Doctrine, Order,* p. 78, William and Norgate, 1882)

It is therefore, quite probable that the followers of the Buddhist faith may have reproduced the whole picture of the Gospels in their books. All such points of resemblance arise from the fact of Jesus' visit to India, which was a piece of good fortune for the followers of the Buddhists' faith from his staying among them for a considerable time.

In my opinion this is the reasonable explanation and a satisfactory answer to the question: 'How did the events of Jesus' life and his teachings creep into Buddhist literature and become ascribed to Gautama Buddha?'

CHAPTER THIRTEEN— YUS ASAPH AND JESUS

This is the last but not the least of the points in connection with the visit of Jesus to India. I have already discussed in the previous pages the statement that Jesus did not die on the cross, but came out of the sepulchre with his body of clay, met his disciples in secret during his stay in Palestine, then, to preach to the lost ten tribes of Israel, went to Nasibin, then to Persia, then to Afghanistan then through the Punjab, reached Kashmir.

The Promised Messiah to whom God revealed that 'The Messiah, Son of Mary, is dead' heard from the inhabitants of Kashmir that in Srinagar, in the Khanyar Street, is a tomb renowned as the tomb of Nabi Sahib (i.e., a prophet). The word *nabi*, which is only used in two languages, Hebrew and Arabic, excited his curiosity and led him to the conclusion that he was a Semitic prophet and preferably a Hebrew prophet, as no prophet appeared from Muslims after the Holy Prophet Muhammad, may peace and blessings of Allah be upon the prophet of God, whose tomb is situated in Medina. Further enquiry confirmed his view, for he was told that the prophet, who was also known by the name of Yus Asaph was a stranger and came to Kashmir some 1900 years ago. These and other factors led him to believe that the buried prophet in Srinagar could be none but Jesus of Nazareth who went to India in search of the tribes of Israel living in these northern regions of India.

Here I relate a few points which support this view:

1. There is oral and written evidence of distinguished people in Srinagar that the occupant of the tomb under discussion was a prophet Yus Asaph who came to Kashmir some 1900 years ago and was also called 'Prince'. A long list of witnesses to this effect is found in the last chapter of *Al-Huda*, an Arabic work by the Promised Messiah, published in 1902 at Qadian.

2. The annals of the country also testify that the tomb is known as that of Prophet Yus Asaph. The author of the *Tarikh-i-Azami* of Kashmir, (historical work written some 200 years ago), referring to this tomb, says, on page 82:

> The tomb next to that of Sayyid Nasr-ud-Din is generally known as that of a prophet who was sent to the inhabitants of Kashmir and the place is known as the shrine of a prophet. He was a prince who came to Kashmir from a foreign land. He was perfect in piety, righteousness, and devotion; he was made a prophet by God and was engaged in preaching to the Kashmiris. His name was Yus Asaph.

3. Rev. Weitbrecht, a Christian missionary, an opponent of the Promised Messiah, who worked for years in the Punjab, after his visit to the tomb in 1903 wrote a letter in a Christian newspaper, *Epiphany*, in which he said:

> Within this are two tombstones. He (a venerable old man in charge of the shrine) said that the larger one at the north end was that of Yus Asaf, and that the smaller tombstone was that of Sayyid Nasr-ud-Din.[a]

4. The Editor of the *Review of Religions*, in the issue dated October, 1909, writes:

> The most remarkable thing about the tomb is that it is known not only as the tomb of a Nabi Sahib, but also as that of Isa Sahib (Jesus). Mirza Bashir-ud-Din Mahmud Ahmad, son of the Promised Messiah, paid a visit to the tomb in July last; and when he asked an old woman (the last survivor of a long line of the hereditary attendants of the tomb) whose tomb it was, she replied: 'It is the tomb of Isa Sahib.' Being asked why she called it the tomb of Isa Sahib, while the Maulvis believed Isa (Jesus) to be in the heavens, she said, 'Let them believe what they will. The name (Isa) is the one which we have been hearing from our forefathers.'

(a) As the Rev. Weitbreeht had misrepresented some facts in his letter, a controversy took place between him and Maulvi Sher Ali, a devout companion of the Promised Messiah, for which refer to *The Review of Religions,* vol. 2, Nos. 11 and 12, 1903; vol 3, No. 5, May, 1904.

5. We read in a book, *Ikmal-ud-Din* (an Arabic work of about 1,000 years ago), on page 359, the following:

> He [Yus Asaph] wandered about in several lands and cities until he reached a land called Kashmir. So he moved about in the land and lived and stayed therein until death overtook him, and he left his body of clay and ascended to the light, and before he breathed his last, he summoned a disciple of his, named Yabid, who used to serve him and wait on his person and was perfect in all matters, and addressed him thus: 'My departure from this world hath drawn nigh; so you must perform your duties and must not swerve from the truth and should observe all rites.' Then he bade the disciple build him a tomb, and stretching out his legs, turned his head to the west and his face to the east, and yielded up the ghost.

Further, we read in this book that Yus Asaph gave the name *Bushra* (Arabic and Hebrew for Gospel) to his message.

> Then he began to compare the tree to *Bushra* (Gospel) which he preached to the people, and he likened a spring of water to the wisdom and knowledge which he possessed, and the birds he compared to the people that swarmed around him and accepted his religion.

6. Sir Francis Younghusband, British Government resident in Kashmir (1909–11), writes:

There resided in Kashmir some 1900 years ago a saint of the name of Yus Asaf, who preached in parables and used many of the same parables as Christ used, as, for instance, the parable of the sower. His tomb is in Srinagar, and the theory of the founder of this Quadiani [sic] Sect is that Yus Asaf and Jesus are one and the same person.[1]

7. One of the points which Dr. Francois Bernier has mentioned in his Travels to show that the Jews lived in Kashmir, is 'the belief that Moses died in the city of Kashmir, and that his tomb is within a league of it. It is obvious that the inhabitants, who, Bernier says, were Muslims, could not say that Moses died in Kashmir and was buried there, because the Holy Prophet of Islam pointed to his tomb in Palestine. It seems that Bernier somehow misunderstood and took Isa for Musa. This point, however, proves beyond doubt that the inhabitants of Kashmir, in the seventeenth century, believed that the occupant of the tomb was a Hebrew Prophet, as great as Moses.[2]

8. Ahmad Islam, after his visit to Kashmir in 1939, wrote in a letter to the editor of *The Sunrise* the following:

I did soon venture out of my room. I mentioned Khanyar to a Tongawala. Spirited was the response. 'You want to see the Rauza of Nabi Sahib, sir?' 'Yes' was my reply, and

---

1. 'Kashmir'—described by Sir Francis Younghusband, p. 129–130. London, 1911.
2. Bernier: *Travels in the Moghul Empire,* p. 430, Oxford University Press.

we were soon on the way. We soon reached the Rauza. I was told that all kinds of visitors, from India and abroad, come to see the tomb. 'Even the Viceroy has been here.' I was interested to hear this. 'Which Viceroy do you mean?' 'Don't know, sir, but I mean the one who did not have an arm.' Evidently it must have been Lord Halifax, the British Foreign Secretary, who was then Lord Irwin. The visit of Lord Halifax was never reported in the papers. At least I do not remember having read anything about it. Still one can understand why Lord Halifax satisfied his curiosity so quietly. Yet a visit by a Viceroy—and as quite unannounced as that—does make it look serious.

'How old, do you think, would be the tomb?'

'Very old, sir.'

'Still, how old?'

The tongawallas, there were three of them, looked at one another, until one of them said 'Nineteen hundred years,' adding he was a prophet who came from somewhere outside. The tomb has been revered for hundreds of years, and this is what we have been hearing from our fathers.[1]

These references to the tomb under discussion show that the entombed person was:
- A prince;
- A *nabi*, i.e., a prophet of God sent to the inhabitants of Kashmir;

---

1. *The Sunrise*, vol. 10. No. 16, April 22, 1939. Lahore, India (now in Pakistan).

- Someone who used to speak in parables;
- A stranger who came from the west some 1900 years ago; and
- Named 'Yus Asaph' and called 'Issa' as well.

Having ascertained these facts, it is not difficult to identify the occupant of the tomb. There has been no prince in the past to whom this distinction might apply other than Prince Jesus the Son of David.

- Jesus was a prince, being called the Son of David[1] whom God exalted to be a prince,[2] and the Prince of the Kings of the earth.[3]
- Jesus was a *nabi*, i.e., a prophet of God to the lost sheep of the House of Israel. He journeyed from Palestine to preach the word of God to the Israelites in Afghanistan and Kashmir.
- Jesus spoke in parables. He called his preaching *Bushra* (Gospel) and compared his disciples to birds. The parable of the sower is mentioned in Matthew (13:3) and 'without a parable spake he not unto them.'[4]
- He travelled from Palestine to Kashmir some 1900 years ago. So the time of the two are the same.
- In the Holy Quran, Jesus' name is *Issa*, shortened form of the Hebrew word *Ishu*.

---

1. Matt. 9:27, 20:30
2. The Acts 5:31
3. Revelation 1:5
4. Matt. 13:34

Yus Asaf

He was called *Yus Asaf* which also is a Hebrew name. The word *Yus* is another form of *Yuyu*, 'Jesus' in the old Persian language, or *Yasu*, 'Jesus' in Persian as well as in the Arabic New Testament translated from the Greek. The word *Yus*, therefore, stands for *Jesus* and *Asaph* is a Biblical name meaning *Collector* or *Gatherer*[a]. We read in 1 Chronicles (16:4–7) that Asaph was a devout Levite, and was appointed chief of the keepers of the Psalms of David.

Jesus' mission was to collect and gather all the scattered tribes of Israel into one fold, as he says:

> And other sheep I have, which are not of this fold: them also must I bring, and they shall hear my voice; and there shall be one fold, *and* one shepherd.[2]

For this reason Jesus was called *Asaf*. When he came to preach to the lost ten tribes in Persia, Afghanistan, and Kashmir, he was rightly called 'Yus Asaf', i.e., 'Jesus Asaf'.

European writers, not knowing the discovery by the Promised Messiah, and basing their opinions on the story of Barlaam and Josaphat or Joasaph, and Christian missionaries especially, to save Jesus from being buried like other prophets, have said that the tomb under discussion is Buddha's. Rev. Weitbrecht, for instance, in his above-mentioned letter has argued that as the events related

---

(a) See Appendix to the Fascimile series of Bagster's polyglot Bible p. 33 under the Index of Proper Names with Meaning.

2. John 10:16

about Yus Asaf in the romance of Barlaam and Josaphat are similar to the events of Buddha's life, the name of Yus Asaf becomes susceptible of explanation and must be another form of Bodhisattva. Likewise Dr. McDonald writes:

> The discovery that the Joasaph or Josaphat of our story was none other than Buddha was made at the same time and independently of one another, by French, German and English scholars. The writer himself admits that the story came from India. Anyone can recognise it as none other than that of Buddha.[1]

Further it is said, 'As a matter of fact, Barlaam is himself a variant of the Buddha, and thus a doublet of Josaphat.'[2]

It should be remembered that the Promised Messiah's source of information concerning the tomb was not the story of Barlaam and Josaphat. However, if the European writers are justified in taking Josaphat for Buddha, it will be equally justifiable for us to take him for Jesus. It should not be forgotten also that the Yus Asaph of Srinagar was a prophet of God, not a mere saint (every prophet is a saint, but not vice versa) or disciple of a prophet. The issue, therefore, lies between the two: the Yus Asaph of Srinagar was either Buddha or Jesus Christ. He cannot be Buddha. Firstly, because Buddha did not die in Srinagar, and his body was not

---

1. Macdonald: *The Story of Barlaam and Joasaph,* Introduction p. iii. Calcutta, 1895.
2. Joseph Jacobs: *Barlaam and Josaphat,* Introduction, p. xiix. London, 1895.

buried, but was cremated. Modern research has discovered the place where Buddha died.

> He died and was cremated at Kusinagara (in Oude) at the age of 80, in the year 543 B.C., his relics distributed among a number of contending claimants, and monumental tombs erected to preserve them.[1]

Dr. T. W. David writes:

> Pre-eminent among these is the discovery by Mr. William Peppe on the Birdpur estate adjoining the boundary between English and Nepalese territory, of the stupa of cairn erected by the Sakia Clan over their share of the ashes from the cremation pyre of the Buddha.[2]

Dr. Herman Oldenberg writes:

> Buddha died in Kusinara. Towards the sunrise the nobles of Kusinara burned Buddha's body before the city gates with all the honours that are shown to the relics of universal monarchs.[3]

It is evident, therefore, that Buddha, who died at Kusinagara or Kusinara, and was cremated, cannot be the occupant of the

---

1. Chambers Encyc. Revised Edition, *Buddhism*. London, 1880.
2. Encyc. Britt. edition *Buddhism*.
3. Oldenberg: *Buddha,* p. 203.

tomb under discussion. Secondly, had the entombed person been Buddha, or any other Hindu Raja, Prince, or Saint, the shrine would have been possessed and visited by Buddhists or Hindus, not by Muslims.

Thirdly: The very name Yus Asaph, as I have discussed above, is a Hebrew name, and it seems ridiculous to take it for another form of Bodhisattva. Is it not more credible that it is another form of Yus Asaph than to take it for a form of Bodhisattva? When it is established that Yus Asaph of Kashmir was not Gautama Buddha then we are justified in saying with full confidence that he was no other than the Prophet Prince, Jesus of Nazareth (peace and blessings of God be upon him).

The genuineness of this discovery by the Promised Messiah, that the entombed Yus Asaph in Srinagar is none other than Jesus, is proved by all possible means by which such events of the distant past are proved, and it is so evident and clear that even Sheikh Rashid Ridha (of Cairo, Egypt), who opposed the Promised Messiah all his life could not help but comment, after reproducing the arguments regarding this tomb, from *Al-Huda* (the Promised Messiah's work in Arabic) in the book *Tafsir-ul-Manar*, vol. 6, under the caption 'Jesus' flight to India and his death in Kashmir', in these words:

> The flight of Jesus, therefore, to India and his death in Srinagar is not foreign to rational or historical truth.

Judge Docker writes:

> I must here notice the old legend which I have before

referred to. A modern version of it was given in the periodical the *East and West*, some years ago. Briefly, it is to the effect that Jesus did not die on the cross, but recovered under treatment with a miraculous ointment being applied to his wounds, which healed in the space of forty days; that he journeyed to India to preach to the lost tribes of Israel, and eventually died at Srinagar, where a tomb is pointed out to this day as his.

Though I do not know of any evidence tending to establish the substantial truth of this account, I desire to point out that there is nothing unreasonable or improbable about it. We are told from other sources that there are to the present day in Afghanistan and Bactria tribes of unmistakable Hebrew type. It is surprising to find the number of passages in the New Testament writings which if they do not corroborate the story, at least are consonant with it. Is it unreasonable then to suppose that Jesus, finding it unsafe to remain in Judea or Galilee longer than the forty days during which he is said to have instructed his disciples in the things concerning the Kingdom of God (Acts 1:3) should feel called to carry the message of the Kingdom to the lost tribes of House of Israel.

Again (page 77) he says:

> I must repeat that we do not know. It may be that after preaching to the lost ten tribes of the House of Israel, in

those remote regions Jesus died at Srinagar, and was buried at the tomb that now bears his name.[1]

John Noel, in an article, *The Heavenly High Snow Peaks of Kashmir*, published in a monthly magazine, *Asia*, October, 1930, U.S.A., writes:

> Immensely strong are the picturesque, broad-shouldered Kashmiri peasants, and yet docile and meek in temperament. One thing about them strikes you with enormous force. They seem more perfectly Jewish than you have ever seen—not because they wear a flowing, cloak-like dress that conforms to your ideas of Biblical garments, but because their faces have the Jewish cast of features.
>
> This curious coincidence, or is it a coincidence,—that there is a strong tradition in Kashmir of connection with the Jews. For a good many years there have been afloat in this land rumours that Christ did not really die upon the cross but was let down and disappeared to seek the lost tribes, that he came to Kashmir, Ladakh, and little Tibet, and died and was buried in Srinagar. Kashmir legend, I have been told, contains reference to a prophet who lived here and taught as Jesus did, by parables—little stories that are repeated in Kashmir to the present day.

Pandit Jawahar Lal Nehru, Premier of India, writes in his book *Glimpses of World History:*

---

1. Docker: *If Jesus did not Die upon the Cross?*, p. 71. London, 1920.

> All over central Asia, in Kashmir and Laddakh and Tibet and even further north, there is still a strong belief that Jesus or Isa travelled about there. (p. 84)

I am confident, therefore, that when those who are endowed with the gift of reason and wisdom will think sincerely, keeping in mind that Jesus came out from sepulchre alive with his wounded mortal body and did not ascend to heaven but lived on earth, will come to the conclusion that the entombed person in Khanyar Street (Srinagar, Kashmir) is Jesus the Son of Mary (peace be upon him).

This is our answer to all those who may ask us: 'If Jesus did not die upon the cross, where did he go and where did he die?'

In this lies the solution to the complicated question about the unknown life of Jesus. If anyone can produce any other solution more credible and reasonable than this, let him come forward and produce it and the world will judge for itself.

Finally I would like to say that were the archaeologists to open the tomb and explore it, they might find some epitaphs upon the stones or other signs in support of the aforesaid discovery, and thus they might redeem hundreds of millions of their fellow beings from worshipping a man who was sent to call the people to the worship of the one and only God.

CHAPTER FOURTEEN—
A PARAMOUNT PROPHECY

The Holy Prophet Muhammad (peace and the blessings of God be upon him) prophesied that the Messiah would appear from amongst the Muslims, in a place east of Damascus, i.e., India; and that he would certainly break the cross, i.e., would prove the falsehood of the Christian doctrine concerning the death of Jesus on the cross, the backbone of the present orthodox Christian faith. As Christian readers may not readily perceive the greatness of this prophecy, I would like to elaborate this point for them.

Before the advent of the Holy Prophet Muhammad (peace and blessings of God be upon him) Jews as well as Christians believed that Jesus died on the cross; the Jews to prove him a false prophet and accursed of God, and the Christians to prove him a person sacrificed by God for the sins of the world, adding that he rose from the dead on the third day, and then, having lived for forty days on earth, ascended to Heaven. Contrary to this belief, God declared in the Holy Quran that Jesus did not die on the cross; and the Holy Prophet explicitly said that 'Jesus died at the age of one hundred and twenty years.'[1] Moreover, on the death of the Holy Prophet all the Muslims confirmed that prophets who had preceded him had all died. When a companion of the Holy Prophet doubted and some others asserted that 'had Muhammad been a prophet of God he would not have died', Hazrat Abu Bakr delivered an address in which he recited the verse from the Holy Quran:

> Muhammad is but a messenger; all messengers before him have passed away; so, if he dies or is killed, will you then turn upon your heels?[2]

On hearing this verse, all the doubts concerning the death of the Holy Prophet vanished from their hearts and they wholeheartedly believed that, like all previous prophets, he too had passed away.

Again, we read in the well-known 'History of the Prophets and Kings' of Abu Jafar Muhammad Ibn Jarir at-Tabari that on the death of the Holy Prophet, the Muslims of Bahrain doubted the truth of the Holy Prophet and turned back to their earlier belief, saying: 'Had Muhammad been a prophet he would not have died.' Jarud, son of Mualla, belonging to the clan of Abdul-Qais, who had acquired adequate religious knowledge during his stay in Medina, put the following question to his tribesmen:

---

1. *Isabah fishur-his-Sahabah*, vol. 5 p. 54, and *Kanz-ul-Ummal*, vol. 7. Reported by Ibn Umar[ra], and Tabarani reports from Hazrat Faatimah[ra].
2. *Bukhari*. Vol. 3, P. 63. Osamaniyya Misriyya Press, 1932.

'Do you know that there were divine prophets in the past?' They replied in the affirmative. He then said: 'Are you only surmising or do you know it?' They answered, 'We indeed know it?' 'Could you tell me then,' he continued, 'what happened to them?' They replied, 'They died.' He said: 'Muhammad died also as they died, and bear witness that there is none worthy to be worshipped but Allah and Muhammad is His messenger.' Following his example, they also said the same, and hailed Jarud their chief.[1]

Thus, they were convinced and became steadfast in Islam. We can see, therefore, that on the death of the Holy Prophet, Muslims understood there was nothing unusual in his death, as prophets before him had also passed away. Thus, the death of Jesus Christ was an undisputed fact accepted by all the companions of the Holy Prophet Muhammad (peace and blessing of God be upon him).

But as time passed, thousands upon thousands of Christians of various countries entered the fold of Islam. Unfortunately, not having adequate knowledge of the Holy Quran and Islamic teachings, these converts still clung to their old traditions and Christian ideas of Jesus Christ which they spread among the Muslims. The latter, relying upon them as co-religionists, took their reports for granted and began to explain the Quranic verses according to these legends. Consequently, the natural death of Jesus upon which all the companions of the Holy Prophet had agreed, was rejected by the Muslims and the belief that Jesus ascended to Heaven in his physical body and that he would descend from Heaven in the

---

1. *Tarikh-ur-Rusul wal-Mulook*, Abu Jafar Muhammad Ibn Jarir at-Tabari.

Latter Days, became so prevalent in the Muslim world, that to speak against it was considered heresy.

> The verse in which Jesus' death on the cross is denied runs thus: And their (i.e., Jews) saying, Surely we have killed the Messiah, Jesus, Son of Mary, the Messenger of Allah, while in fact they did not kill him, but it was made dubious to them, (i.e.,) he appeared to them as one dead ... and they surely did not kill him. Nay! Allah exalted him and bestowed upon him the gift of nearness to Him, and Allah is Mighty, Wise.[1]

In view of this clear statement that the Jews did not kill Jesus, no Muslim could possibly say that Jesus died on the cross. The Muslims, therefore, on the one hand accepted the report of their co-believers converted from Christianity, that the person who was fixed to the cross actually died and on the other, denied that this person was Jesus Christ. They said that when Jesus was detained in a room by the Jews, God sent His angel who lifted him up to Heaven through a skylight, and the guard was made as the like of Jesus, and the crucifiers took this substitute and crucified him. Some of the Muslim commentators have gone so far as to say that Jesus died a natural death for three days and then ascended to Heaven. The idea that another man was made to resemble Christ is not found in the Holy Quran nor is it supported by a single saying of the Holy Prophet. All the legends concerning it are unauthorised and unreliable.

---

1. Jarir, *At-Tabari,* p. 1058–59. Brill 1890.

Moreover, we do not see any sense in making another man resemble Jesus, and then handing him over to the Jews. If God had lifted Jesus up to Heaven, what need was there of presenting the supposed substitute to the Jews? Did God want to console the Jews that they might boast they had killed Jesus and prove him a cursed one? Again, it is nowhere stated that the substitute ever tried to deny being Jesus Christ. He could easily have proved this and escaped. At least any of his friends or relatives, seeing he had disappeared, would have made a search for him. If this story is true, then Jews could not be justifiably condemned for believing Jesus to be an impostor and a false prophet. They did not see him soaring up to Heaven, and the substitute made to appear as Jesus, did not even deny being the Messiah, and the Jews crucified him believing that he was Jesus himself. The Jews, in this case therefore, will be excused in the sight of God for rejecting Jesus. But this is directly at variance with the gist of the verse under discussion, as it says that the Jews are under the curse of God because they say that they caused him to die on the cross.

Besides this verse, there are many other verses in the Holy Quran which clearly show that Jesus died a natural death. For instance, we read in the Holy Quran, that when Allah will question Jesus, 'Did you say to the people that they should take you and your mother for two gods besides Me,' he would answer, 'Glory be to Thee, it does not befit me to say what I had no right to say...I said to them naught but what Thou hadst commanded me: saying, 'Serve Allah my Lord and your Lord' and I was a witness over them as long as I was amongst them; but when Thou didst cause me to die,

Thou wast the Watcher over them, and Thou art a Witness over all things.'[1]

It is evident from this verse that Jesus, when he will be questioned by God on the Day of Resurrection, will declare that he died a natural death at the time when there existed no idea of his 'Divinity' among the Christians. The popular belief that Jesus is still alive in Heaven and that he will come to earth again is in direct contradiction with this verse. For if he were to come to earth again he would be faced with the fact that millions of Christians take him as God. Thus, he would not be in a position to deny that he did not see Christians believe in his 'Divinity' as this verse declares he would. However, the fact that Jesus though fixed to the cross, did not die on it, but died a natural death remained hidden from the Muslims for centuries, until the Promised Messiah appeared and uncovered the truth. In his book, *Masih Hindustan Mein* (Chapter 2), the Promised Messiah, comments on the verse denying the death of Jesus on the cross:

> "Almighty God says: The Jews neither slew Jesus, nor did they crucify him"[(a)] (i.e., made him die on the cross); nay, they only suspected that Jesus had died on the cross;

---

1. The Holy Quran, ch. 5, vs. 116–117
2. The Muslim commentators misunderstood from the Quranic word *Ma salabooho* that they did not *fix* Jesus to the cross, therefore they denied the fact that he was placed on the cross. While the word *sulb* in Arabic has exactly the same meaning as the English word *'to crucify'* i.e., to put to death by fixing the hands and feel to a cross. (*Chambers' Twentieth Century Dictionary*). The sentence *Salabuhu* means, he put him to death in a certain well-known manner. (Lane's Arabic-English lexicon).

they had not the proofs which would have convinced and satisfied them that Jesus (on whom be peace) had really died on the cross. In the verses Almighty God says that although it is true that Jesus was placed on the cross, and that they were determined to kill him, it is wrong for Jews and Christians to suppose that Jesus had really died on the cross; nay, God created circumstances which saved Jesus from death on the cross. If one is just, one must say that what the Holy Quran had said against what the Jews and Christians had believed turned out to be true. A modern investigator of high merit has proved that Jesus was saved from death on the cross. A study of written record shows that Jews had never been able to reply to the question: 'How was it that Jesus died within two or three hours, when his bones had not been broken?' This led the Jews to manufacture the plea that they had killed Jesus with the sword; whereas the ancient history of the Jews does not say that Jesus had been killed by the sword. It was due to the Majesty and Power of God that it became dark, that there was an earthquake, that Pilate's wife saw a vision, that the Sabbath night was about to fall, when it was unlawful to let the crucified body remain on the cross, and that the magistrate, because of the dream of his wife became inclined to release Jesus. All this was brought about by God to save Jesus. Also Jesus was made to go into a swoon that he might be taken for dead.

The terrible signs, the earthquake, etc., produced in the Jews the fear of heavenly punishment. Besides there was the apprehension lest the corpses should remain on the cross during the Sabbath night. The Jews, seeing Jesus in a swoon, thought he was dead. It was dark, there was an earthquake and great excitement. They also became anxious about their homes: how must the children be feeling in that darkness and earthquake?

There was terror in their hearts, that if this man was a liar and a heretic, why were such terrible signs manifested, at the time of his suffering? Signs which had never been manifested before? They were so upset that they were no longer in a position to satisfy themselves whether Jesus had in fact died, or what exactly his condition was.

What had happened, however, was really a divine design to save Jesus. This is hinted at in the verse *Walakin shubbiha lahum,* i.e., the Jews did not kill Jesus, God made them think they had killed him. The circumstance encourages the righteous to place trust in God: He can save His servants as He likes.

Again the Promised Messiah[as] says in the same book:

I, however, do not approve of the way of European investigators who wish to prove, somehow or other, that the principles of Buddhism had reached Palestine in the days of Jesus. It is a matter of regret that as the name of Jesus is mentioned in the ancient books of Buddhism, investigators should adopt the awkward course of finding traces of Buddha's faith in Palestine. Why not search for the blessed footprints of Jesus on the rocky soil of Nepal, Tibet, and Kashmir?

But these investigators could not be expected to discover the truth, hidden under a thousand coverings of darkness. It was the work of God who saw from the heavens that man-worship, overstepping all limits, had spread over the world and that the worship of the Cross and of the supposed sacrifice of a human being had alienated many millions of people from the True God whose jealousy sent to the world a servant of His in the name of Jesus of Nazareth, to break the creed of the Cross. In accordance with the ancient promise, therefore, he appeared as the Promised Messiah. Then came the time for the breaking of the Cross, i.e., the time when the error of the creed of the Cross was to be made plain. The idea of Jesus going up to Heaven, though it was an error, had, nevertheless, a secret. The Messianic reality had been forgotten and had gone out of existence, even as a corpse is eaten up by the earth of the grave. This Messianic reality was believed to be in existence in the heavens in the corporeal form of human being. It was inevitable, therefore, that this reality should descend to the earth in the Latter Days. So it has descended to the earth in this age in the shape of a living human being, and it has broken the Cross. Do not think therefore, that I have come with a sword. No, I have come to put all swords back into their scabbards. The world has been fighting a good deal in darkness. Many a man has attacked his true well-wishers, wounded the hearts of sympathetic friends, and injured his dear ones, but now the darkness is no more. Night is gone and the day is come and blessed is he who remains deprived no longer.

Thus has been fulfilled what was prophesied by the Holy Prophet Muhammad (peace and the blessings of God be upon him) nearly 1,350 years ago, that the Promised Messiah would break the Cross and show the falsehood of the belief in Jesus' death on the cross. It has also fulfilled what was said by Jesus himself that at the time of his second advent: 'shall all the tribes of the earth mourn'.[1] It means Christians, Jews, and Muslims who are inhabitants of the earth (i.e., Palestine) shall be sorry when they learn their beliefs about Jesus have been false.

As in the third century A.D., at the time of Constantine, the cross was publicly taken as a symbol of Christian religion, likewise God has foretold through the mouth of the Promised Messiah that all Crosses will be broken when Christians realise the falsity of their belief:

> The third century from this day shall not pass until all those who look for the descent of Jesus from heaven, Christians or Muslims will despair of it and will forsake the false beliefs now so fondly cherished by them. Then there will be one religion in the world and one leader. I have been sent to sow a seed and I have sown it. It will now grow and bear flowers and fruit in due season and there is none who can uproot it.[2]

Before I close I should like to pray in the words of the Promised Messiah, the Prophet of this age, sent by God to fulfil the prophecies of the prophets of various nations. He says:—

---

1. Matt. 24:30
2. Ahmad, The Promised Messiah. *Tazkirat-ush-Shahadatain*, p. 65; Qadian, 1903.

Our beloved Allah, save the Christians from worshipping a man as God, and fulfil the promises of Thy prophets for this age. Lift the wounded ones from the thorns. Purify them in the fountain of Thy salvation which lies only in Thy knowledge and Thy love. There is no salvation in the blood of man. Merciful God, it has been long that Christians have worshipped a man, but now have mercy on them, and open their eyes. Almighty and Merciful God, everything is possible unto Thee. Release them, therefore, from the false dogmas of the crucifixion and the blood of Jesus. Almighty God, hear me for their benefit, and enlighten their hearts with heavenly light so that they may see Thee. Who can imagine they would see Thee? In whose mind would they avoid the worshipping of a creature, and listen to Thy voice? But O God, everything is possible for Thee. So do not destroy them as Thou didst in the days of Noah. After all they are Thy creatures. Have mercy upon them. Open their hearts so that they may accept the Truth.

J. D. SHAMS,
London, March 14, 1945
Imam of the London Mosque

APPENDIX TO SIXTH EDITION

(Taken from the *Sunday Times*, London, January 24, 1965)

In 1955 Dr. J. G. Bourne, a senior anaesthetist of St. Thomas's Hospital and Salisbury Hospital Group, began investigating cases of patients fainting under general anaesthesia in the dentist's chair. This can cause death: a man kept upright in a faint loses blood-supply to the brain. Dr. Bourne published this original research in 1957. Later, turning over his discoveries in his mind, he began to relate certain aspects to the facts of the Crucifixion and Resurrection. The theory that resulted was somewhat startling, but Dr. Bourne, himself a man of strong Christian belief, feels that it could make Christianity more attractive to people unable to accept the supernatural explanation of the Resurrection. He quotes the Archbishop of Canterbury, who wrote on the Resurrection: 'There is need for the most scientific approach to historical proof that is possible'. This is an abbreviated version of

Dr. Bourne's paper on his theory, which is to be published elsewhere in more technical form.

Normally, discussion of the Resurrection centres on the historical proofs (now generally accepted) of Jesus' subsequent appearances on earth. To question His actual death may be thought heresy—but there is reason to think that Jesus in fact fainted on the cross, was believed dead, and recovered after a period of coma.

Dr. C. C. P. Clark, writing in the New York 'Medical Record' in 1908 suggested that Jesus' apparent death might have been a fainting attack. In 1935 Professor S. Weiss, an American authority on fainting, pointed out that fainting was the usual cause of death in victims of crucifixion, and this is now accepted among medical scientists.

The essential feature of fainting is a fall in arterial blood pressure, caused by active dilatation of the smaller arteries of the body, mainly in the muscles. Blood then gets away from the arterial side of the circulation with greatly decreased resistance. At the same time the heart is slowed, and may stop for several seconds.

The onset may come without warning, though not usually, and there may be a sense of impending death.

Blood pressure falls precipitously, the brain's oxygen supply is reduced, consciousness is lost and the subject falls down. Breathing is shallow, the pupils are dilated, and the appearance death-like: not even the deepest coma so closely resembles death.

The abolition of muscle power which causes the fall is a safeguard to the brain, which is readily damaged by oxygen-lack. In the horizontal position, blood pressure is restored, and consciousness returns. However, deathly pallor may continue for an hour or more—due to release of pituitary hormone, part of the reflex response.

If the subject is kept upright: (a) blood pressure may spontaneously return above fainting-level; (b) the subject may recover momentarily and faint again, perhaps repeatedly; (c) he may continue in the faint, with progressively falling blood pressure, but still with a survival chance; or he may die instantaneously because the heart stopped beating at the onset and did not resume. In fatal cases, however, death is usually due to brain damage from lack of oxygen, and may come in two or three minutes, or be delayed even for weeks.

Recovery

Depending on the blood pressure level and the length of time he is kept upright, the survivor may suffer stupor or coma, with recovery after a few hours or days, various degrees of permanent intellectual impairment, or profound dementia and delayed death. Such cases are not uncommon in medicine.

Some years ago, investigation was made by the writer into certain accidents which occurred in dentistry and discovered that patients, under light anaesthesia with nitrous-oxide, might develop a fainting attack. [Dr. Bourne published this research in his book 'Nitrous Oxide in Dentistry'.] Under a general anaesthetic, this was unnoticed until, quite suddenly, the patient developed all the appearances of being dead. At that time the importance of getting the patient flat was not understood, and when eventually lifted from the chair to the floor, he would lie pallid and inert until consciousness slowly returned. Many such cases were discovered: the coma lasting half an hour, several hours, a day or two, or in one extreme case, two weeks. Some cases were fatal.

Information having been collected of more than 100 cases in the dental field, and others not related to anaesthesia, they appeared as a series of events remarkably like the Crucifixion and Resurrection.

Walking

The Crucifixion (according to the Gospels and Renan's 'Life of Jesus') took place around noon, and Jesus' apparent death occurred suddenly about 3 p.m. He was taken down and laid in the tomb, but at dawn on Sunday, forty hours later, was no longer there. Five times that day He was seen walking and talking to people: first with Mary Magdalene, just after dawn, who initially did not recognise Him. He also had a long discourse with disciples before being recognised.

The period that the upright position could be held in a faint and allow recovery of consciousness after relatively few hours' coma would depend on how low blood-pressure fell: this determining the degree of the brain's oxygen-lack. The level in his case cannot be guessed, but it seems the fainting-interval on the cross was short. Some advantage would be gained by the fact that on fainting the head would fall forward, thus lessening the distance from heart to brain, and improving blood flow. St. John says the Jews did not want the bodies to remain on the cross for the coming Sabbath so they asked Pilate to have them taken down. The soldiers accordingly came to the first of his fellow victims and to the second, and broke their legs; but when they came to Jesus, they found that he was already dead, so they did not break his legs. But one of the soldiers stabbed his side with a lance, and at once there was a flow of blood and water.

Sympathetic

The soldiers were acting under Pilate's orders, and presumably would have forthwith taken down the bodies. (The centurion, sympathetic to Jesus, would probably have seen that it was done promptly). Renan says that when Joseph asked Pilate for Jesus' body, it had already been taken down. It is certain that the soldiers did not break his legs—the usual method of applying the coup-de-grace to victims.

Next, how did it happen that blood flowed from the wound? In a dead body, blood will ooze from cut veins, but there is not the flow of blood suggested by St. John's description. (In operating for cardiac arrest, a flow would rightly be taken as evidence that the heart was still beating, and the surgeon would not proceed to open the chest.) In fainting, this is just what would be expected, with the small muscle arteries dilated. The lance could hardly have failed to pierce muscle, and the wound was probably well below heart level, where blood pressure would be appreciable even in a faint.

Apart from the likeness of the faint to death, death is not always easily diagnosed: mistakes are made even today. I know personally of two persons pronounced dead by doctors after careful examination who revived in the mortuary—one of them left hospital thirteen days later on foot. In Jesus, death appears to have been diagnosed by soldiers: what could be more understandable than a mistake during the tumult of this terrible event?

Changed

Nor is it surprising that close associates should have failed initially to recognise Jesus afterwards. He would have looked an ill man, much changed. It might be argued that during the post-Crucifixion period, His words lacked somewhat their former vigour and brilliance: can it be that cerebral anoxia on the cross had left its mark?

A great many people must have doubted the reality of Jesus' death upon the cross, or else the literal truth of the Resurrection. That He fainted, and did not die was suggested by Dr. Clark, three-quarters of a century ago, and according to Renan, recovery after crucifixion was known to the ancients. If there was nothing supernatural about the reappearance of Jesus, need that be an obstacle to the acceptance of His teachings? His life is sublime without physical myths: nothing can take away the miracles of the spirit.

APPENDIX TO SEVENTH EDITION

Further Evidence and the Latest Theories

The Sixth Edition was updated with latest available comments to 1965, and a similar opportunity has been taken to update the Seventh Edition. It goes without saying that research about to be conducted on the Holy Shroud of Turin in 1978 will encourage seekers of truth to seek fresh venues in examining this subject with closer scrutiny.

Dr. Pierre Barbet

In 1931, Dr. Pierre Barbet, a French surgeon and anatomist, was approached for counsel by Father Armailhac on the set of photographs of the Shroud taken by Enrie. In 1950, Dr. Barbett published *La Passion de N.S. Jesus Christ selon le Chirugien* (its English translation is titled 'A Doctor at Calvary'). His research concluded as follows:

1. The blood which flowed from the wounds coagulated on the skin and was transferred to the cloth by direct contact on the Shroud.

2. He observed as many as 120 wounds caused by the striking of a double-thonged flagrum which caused scourging on the body.

3. Marks caused by the crown of thorns, wounds caused by carrying the crucifix and appearing on the left shoulder blade, across the right shoulder and the knees could not have been faked on the Shroud.

4. Nails were driven not through the palms but through the fleshy space bounded by bones in the wrist. By studying the angle of flow of blood from the wrist wounds, he determined that the body had alternately taken two different positions on the cross indicating that the body had raised itself slightly from time to time, using the feet as a fulcrum.

5. Death was caused through asphyxiation and tetany. According to the doctor, the blade of the lance had entered the body above the sixth rib, penetrated the pleura (a serous membrane enveloping the lung), the right lung, puncturing the pericardium (a membranous sac enclosing the heart) and finally piercing the right auricle of the heart itself. Blood flowed from the inferior

vena cava into the abdomen. When the body was carried in a horizontal position, the blood of inferior vena cava would have flowed back into the right auricle, passing through the tunnel made by the lance and eventually flowing out, slipping around the right side going right across the lower part of the thorax. As this opinion was given by a Christian on commission to a friendly clergyman, some doubt must be cast on the independence of objectives; experiments were done on cadavers and death was taken for granted. In a vertical position on the cross, blood not coagulated would have naturally flown downwards into the abdomen and the evidence given by John 'and at once there was a flow of blood and water' would have remained unanswered.

Professor Hirt contradicts this by stating that blood only flows from a living body as otherwise the heart ceases to function and there is no blood pressure to make blood flow. There is evidence of blood serum exudate on the Shroud and the stains of blood from the back of the head and neck on the shroud could have only been caused when the wound was re-opened from a living body.

When this basis was rejected, Sava conjectured that the lance may have passed between the fifth and the sixth ribs so that serous fluid and bloody effusion in the pleural cavity of the lungs would have caused blood and water to flow. There is absolutely no medical evidence to suggest that the lance may have penetrated a well-protected heart. The space between the fifth and sixth ribs at an acute angle from lower below would have been insufficient for deep penetration. The angle of the blow and that of the body positively suggest that the spear definitely missed the heart (as has been shown by X-ray experiments) and at the most may have just brushed the lungs. The healing qualities of myrrh and aloe contain a sealing agent which would have been used to help the 2 to 3 inch wound heal. Again, serous fluid in the pleural cavity protected by the pleural membrane should have followed the law of gravity and remained within the body.

Dr. Nicu Haas

In June, 1968, Israeli builders excavated three burial graves containing human skeletal remains. Outside one tomb were two inscriptions bearing the name Jehohanan who met his death by crucifixion. Dr. Nicu Haas of the Department of Anatomy, Hebrew University-Hadassah Medical School, found evidence to suggest that a nail was driven between the radius and ulna (bones of the forearm) and that the victim must have writhed in anguish towards the end of his ordeal. The lower leg bones (the tibiae and the left fibula) were fractured as a result of a direct and deliberate blow to the leg as a coup de grace of crucifragium which insured rapid death. 'The feet were joined almost parallel, both transfixed by the same nail at the heels, with the legs adjacent.' This is similar to the image appearing on the Shroud of Turin, although Jesus was spared crucifragium. The foot-rest is of particular importance as it delayed death by suffocation on the cross.

Image on the Shroud

1. Vapograph Theory

Paul Vignon advanced the theory that the image on the Shroud was caused by ammoniacal vapours acting on the aloe-impregnated cloth. Although Paul Vignon has been his own self-critic, his theory has not been disproved.

However, Professor Hirt suggests that the stains could only be caused by active flowing of blood directly on the Shroud. His theory remains undisputed because blood which has coagulated on the skin cannot produce a stain with serous marking around it.

2. Direct Contact Theories

- Dr. Giovanni Judica-Cordigilia was able to produce images with negative characteristics by moistening a corpse with blood, covering it with a strip of linen soaked in a solution of olive oil, turpentine, mixed with aloes and exposing the linen-draped body to hot steam in the presence of light.
- Dr. R. Romanese was able to reproduce similar crude images by dampening a corpse with a solution of physiological salt and sprinkling linen with powdered salt before exposing it to light.
- Dr. P. Scotti made an emulsion of aloes in olive oil and after simple contact with air caused the aloetine-soaked cloth to form images which were extremely faint at first but which darkened with time after exposure to sunlight. It is possible that John

makes no reference to any images on the cloth because they were not so profound then, but matured with time.

These theories require the anointing of the Shroud with some kind of aromatic that facilitated a chemical reaction. Above all, they require conditions synonymous to a living body before images are formed, and should the Shroud be authentic, there will be little doubt to believe that it wrapped the body of a living Christ.

Between 1897–1902, Albert Gayert, unearthed excavations at Antinoe, a town built on the Nile in Egypt by the Roman Emperor Hadrian in A.D. 132. One of the Christian bodies unearthed had undergone shroud burial with 'a face veil, folded in four, that bears the apparently undistorted imprint of the dead person's face, similar to the Shroud's death mask. The experts think that this fourfold impression was made by some chemical process involving spices.'

The author has already quoted in Chapter 4 an eyewitness account by an Essene brethren in a letter to a fellow-brother in Egypt. Is it not possible that this letter is now all the more authentic in view of this Egyptian discovery of a similar shroud?

Authenticity of the Shroud

The authenticity of the Shroud of Turin has further been proved by:

1. Dr. Max Frie, a criminologist and pollen analysis specialist.

The pollen dust of every plant can be identified. In 1973, he took 12 samples from the linen fibres 10–12 cms. long and studied these at Zurich under a microscope. By studying and comparing pollen from various geographical regions, he concluded that the Shroud was at some time exposed to the Palestinian and Turkish areas. It is not possible to date when this exposure took place.

2. Christian historians have doubted the authenticity of the Shroud because no mention is made of this cloth. However, Muslim historians like Al-Masudi and Ibn-ul-Athir link it to King Abgarus of Edessa before it arrived in Christian hands (see the *Muslim Herald*, Vol. 18, No. 1, January, 1978).

3. Dr. John P. Jackson and Dr. Eric Jumper of the U.S. Air Force Academy have studied the intensity of darkness of the stains and plotted a graph showing body to cloth distance on a microdensometer and reinterpreting this on an image analyser. This technique is similar to the space research programme whereby three-dimensional reliefs are obtained. The clarity of these images indicate that the Shroud could not have been faked.

The original Greek version of the Gospels merely use the words 'the giving up of the ghost'. Death is not mentioned. At that time, the cessation of breathing was assumed to be 'death'. Present day medicine, however, requires that efforts for revival should be continued even if a person has stopped breathing and there are hundreds of patients who owe their 'new' lives to this fundamental recognition of death in the medical terminology.

The search for a historical Christ carries on. It needs to be elevated, however, because Jesus Christ was a prophet of God who was in receipt of divine revelation. He was, nonetheless, a human being prone to death. It is a great miracle of God that he was saved from the cross and died a natural death. The admission of this basic fact satisfies the historian and satisfies all those who believe in prophethood. Those who do not believe in this, but wish to credit Jesus with God-like powers, will have to manufacture a lot more lies to satisfy the demand by the average seeker of truth to whom truth needs to be presented in its raw and simple form.

May God Almighty guide us to truth. Amen!

APPENDIX
TO TWELFTH EDITION

The Nag Hammadi Library

It is absolutely astonishing that the Holy Prophet Muhammad[saw]—an illiterate man living amidst a nation notorious for its ignorance—could so confidently oppose the beliefs of the Jews and Christians, despite their academic prestige, pomp, and power. At a time when the overwhelming majority of Jews and Christians were content to condemn Jesus[as] to an accursed death, the Holy Prophet[saw] glorified Christ stating that God had revealed to him that Jesus[as] did not die on the cross; rather, he only *appeared* to have died on the cross [Quran 3:158]. God saved Jesus[as] from that accursed death and exalted him to Himself in spiritual rank, whereas his enemies deluded themselves into believing the conjecture that they succeeded in killing him in a manner that proved he was false [Quran 3:56]. In this way the Holy Prophet[saw] fulfilled Jesus' prophecy of the Promised Comforter:

> ...he will guide you into all truth: for he shall not speak of himself; but whatsoever he shall hear, that shall he speak: and he will shew you things to come. He shall glorify me... [John 16:13–14]

Jesus[as] alluded to the same message of the Quran when he stated that the sign of Jonah[as] was the only sign for his generation [Matt 16:4]. Just as Jonah[as] *appeared* to drown, so did Jesus[as] *appear* to die on the cross; and just as Jonah[as] survived, 'rising from the drowned', so too would Jesus[as] survive, 'rising from the dead'.

Although the initial statements of the Holy Prophet[saw] and the Promised Messiah[as] were primarily attributable to their revelations, God Himself would reveal additional evidence in the future to further corroborate the Quranic statement that Jesus[as] survived the Crucifixion. In addition to Maulana Jalal-ud-Din Shams' research, one recent example of such evidence includes the discovery of the Nag Hammadi Library in 1945 consisting of over 50 texts, many of which were thought to have been destroyed prior to this extraordinary discovery. According to best-selling author and Princeton professor Elaine Pagels, these texts date to the earliest centuries of Christianity and reveal a far greater range of Christian diversity as the faith struggled to identify what would eventually become its Orthodoxy. These texts—remaining virtually untouched for 1500 years—were translated in the 1970s and present a rich source to cross-examine modern-day Christian beliefs, even though today's Orthodoxy conveniently labels their authors as heretics.

In 'The Gnostic Bible', published in 2006 by New Seeds Books (Boston, Massachusetts) and edited by Willis Barnstone and Marvin Meyer, we find several references that harmonize with the Promised Messiah's belief that Jesus[as] did not die on the cross and later departed to another land. The following are a sample of such references and are written in first person, as if the author is Jesus[as] himself:

They surrounded me like mad dogs
who stupidly attack their masters.
... I didn't perish...
They sought my death. They failed. ...
They cast lots against me. They failed.

[Songs of Solomon, Response to Song 28]

I stretched out my hands and came near my lord.
It is my sign, stretching my hands as if spread on a tree.
That was my way up to the good one.
I became useless to those who didn't seize me.
I hid from those who don't love me
but am with them who love me.
My persecutors died.
They sought me because I am alive.
I rose up and am with them
and speak through their mouths.
...They thought me rejected, destroyed. I wasn't. ...

[Songs of Solomon, Song 42]

And I was in the mouth of lions. And as for the plan that they devised about me to release their error and their senselessness, I did not succumb to them as they had planned. And I was not afflicted at all. Those who were there punished me, yet I did not die in reality but in appearance, in order that I not be put to shame by them because these are my kinsfolk... I suffered merely according to their sight and thought so that no word might ever be found to speak about them. For my death, which they think happened, happened to them in their error and blindness, since they nailed their man unto their death. Their thoughts did not see me, for they were deaf and blind. But in doing these things, they condemn themselves.

[The Second Treatise of the Great Seth]

Some say the lord died first and then ascended.
They are wrong. He rose first and then he died. ...

[The Gospel of Philip]

A literal reading of some of the above references may give the impression that someone else was crucified instead of Jesus[as], but in the deeply metaphoric idiom of Hebrew, Aramaic and Syriac, this can simply mean that the Jews misled themselves into believing that Christ died the accursed death they planned for him, and that misconception materialized into the man they crucified; whereas the man that God saved was someone quite different from their misperception: altogether exonerated and glorified from that shameful death. In other words, there were not two different men, but two different beliefs about the same man, each taking a life of its own, so to speak.

The following references indicate that Jesus[as] may have spent a substantially greater amount of time with the Disciples and other close followers—as opposed to the mere forty days mentioned in Acts 1:3—after which he would depart from them:

> Five hundred fifty days after he rose from the dead, we said to him, 'Did you depart and leave us?'
>
> [The Secret Book of James]

> *The students said to Yeshua,*
> *We know you will leave us.*
> *Who will be our leader?*
> *Yeshua said to them,*
> *Wherever you are, seek out Yaakov the just* [i.e., James the Just]...
>
> [The Gospel of Thomas, Saying 12]

> Since I was glorified like this once before, why do you hold me back when I am eager to go? After my labor you have made me stay with you another eighteen days [or emended to 'months' per the editor's suggestion] because of the parables...
>
> Look, I shall be leaving you and go away. I do not want to stay with you any longer just as you yourselves have not wanted this.
>
> [The Secret Book of James]

Once again, it is simply astonishing that the above references—from scriptures protected from Orthodox tampering for centuries—bear a strong resemblance to the teachings within the Holy Quran.

On the other hand, the Orthodox Christian version leaves us little satisfaction of the post-Crucifixion narration of events. During the forty day period after the Crucifixion [Acts 1:3], we hardly have any record of Jesus' activities. One would expect the witnesses around Jesus to be so amazed at his miraculous survival that they would record every single statement he spoke, trusting that he was no ordinary man; but they record hardly anything in comparison to the volumes they recorded of his pre-Crucifixion activities, when his true status was yet unknown and subject to doubt.

To add to this frustration, only two of the four Gospel 'eyewitness' accounts [Mark and Luke] record Jesus[as] as physically ascending to the right hand of the Father [i.e., God]; yet scriptural evidence has proven even those to be interpolations. Constantin von Tischendorf [1815 C.E. to 1874 C.E.] was a renowned German Biblical scholar who made one of the greatest scriptural discoveries in Christian history: The Codex Sinaiticus. Tischendorf discovered the Codex Sinaiticus in St. Catharine's Monastery located in the Sinai Peninsula. This Codex is the oldest most complete New Testament that exists to date. Interestingly enough, when looking at the Gospels of Mark and Luke in the Codex Sinaiticus, their accounts end before any mention of the Ascension, proving the Ascension was a later interpolation and fabrication.

BIBLIOGRAPHY

1. *The Holy Quran.*

2. *Sahih-ul-Bukhari*, Collection of the sayings of the Holy Prophet, edition I (Osmaniyya Misriyya Press Egypt, 1932).

3. *Kanz-ul-Ummal* by Sheikh Ala-ud-Din (Hyderabad 1214 AH).

4. *Masih Hindustan Mein* ['Jesus in India'] by Mirza Ghulam Ahmad, the Promised Messiah[as] (Qadian, 1889).

5. *Tazkirat-ush-Shahadatain* by Mirza Ghulam Ahmad, the Promised Messiah[as] (Qadian, 1908).

6. *Isabah fi Shur-his-Sahabah.*

7. *Tarikh-ur-Rusul wal-Mulook* by Abu Jafar Muhammad Ibn Jarir-at-Tabari (Brill, 1890).

8. *The Bible* (King James Version).

9. *Dictionary of the Bible* by Sir William Smith and the Rev. J. M. Fuller (London, 1893).

10. *The Quest of the Historical Jesus* by Albert Schweitzer (Translated by W. Montgomery. London, Black, 1911).

11. *If Jesus did not Die upon the Cross?* A Study in *Evidence* by Ernest Brougham Docker, District Court Judge, Sydney (London, Robert Scott, 1920).

12. *Encyclopaedia Britannica* 11th and 14th Editions.

13. *Jewish Encyclopaedia.*

14. *Chamber's Encyclopaedia.* Revised edition (London, W. and R. Chambers, High Street, Edinburgh, 1880).

15. *The Age of Reason* by Thomas Paine based directly upon that of Daniel Isaac Eatons' editions of 1795 and 1796 (London, Watt and Co., 1938).

16. *The Paganism in our Christianity,* by Arthur Weigall (Hutchinson and Co,, Publishers, Ltd).

17. *Adonis, Attis and Osiris* (edition 2), by Sir James Frazer (Macmillan and Co., Ltd., London, 1907).

18. *The Golden Bough* (Part 6), by Sir James Frazer (London. 1913).

19. *The 'Watchman' Magazine* (London, March, 1940).

20. *The Book of Common Prayer.*

21. *Through Bible Lands* by Phillip Schaff (London, James Nisbet, 1888).

22. *A Complete Concordance to the Holy Scriptures* by Alexander Cruden.

23. *The Life and Times of Jesus the Messiah* by Alfred Ede-sheim, London, Longmans Green and Co., 1886.

24. *The Races of Afghanistan* by Surgeon-Major H. W. Bellewes (Calcutta, Thacker, Spink and Co., 1886).

25. *A New Afghan Question, or Are the Afghans Israelites?* by Surgeon-Major H. W. Bellews (Cradock and Co., Simla, 1880).

26. *The History of Christianity in India from the Commencement of the Christian Era* by the Rev. James Hough, Vol. 2 (published by R. B. Seeley and W. Burnside, and sold by L. and G. Seeley, Shaftesbury Avenue, London, 1839).

27. *Dictionary of Geography,* by A. Keith Johnstone (London, Longmans Green, 1867).

28. *Travels in the Moghul Empire* A.D. 1656–1668' by Francois Bernier, translated by Archibald Constable (1891). 2nd edition revised by Vincent A. Smith (Humphrey Milphord, Oxford University Press, 1941).

29. *Kashmir—Described by Sir Francis Younghusband, K.C.I.E.,* printed by Major E. Molyneux, London, and Black, 1909).

30. *The History of the Beni Israel of India* by Heem Samuel Kehimkar, (published by the Dayag Press Ltd., Tel-Aviv, 1937. London Agent: George Sablby).

31. *The Spectator*, London, No. 5634, June 19th, 1936.

32. *Great Britain and the East,* London, December 3rd, 1936.

33. *The Works of Flavius Josephus,* Whiston's translation with notes by Sir C. W. Wilson', London, 1889.

34. *A General Collection of the Best and Most Interesting Voyages and Travels in all Parts of the World,* by John Pinkerton, London, 1811, (Vol. 7.) Printed for Longmans, etc.

35. *The Unknown Life of Jesus Christ* by the discoverer of the manuscripts, Nicolas Notovitch (Translated from the French by Alexina Loranger. (Rand, NcNally and Co., Chicago and New York, 1894).

36. *The Story of Barlaam and Joasaph, Buddhism and Christianity,*

edited by K. S. Macdonald (Calcutta, Thacker, Spink and Co., 1895).

37. *Lectures on Buddhism* (3rd edition), by Ernest J. Eitel (London, 1884).

38. *Buddha: His Life, Doctrine, His Order,* by Hermann Oldenberg, Professor of the University of Berlin. Translated from the German by William Hoey (Published by the Book Co. Ltd., Calcutta, 1927; and William and Norgate, 1882).

39. *The Sunrise* (Weekly publication, Lahore).

40. *Asia* (Monthly magazine published in USA).

41. *Barlaam and Josephat* by Jacobs (Published by David Nutt, Shaftesbury Avenue, London, 1897).

42. *Review of Religions* (Monthly magazine, Qadian). I have taken a few passages, with slight alterations, from various numbers of this publication.

PUBLISHER'S NOTE

Salutations are recited out of respect when mentioning the names of Prophets and holy personages. These salutations have been abbreviated and inserted into the text where applicable. Readers are urged to recite the full salutations for the following abbreviations:

saw   *Sallallaahu 'alaihi wa sallam,* meaning 'May peace and blessings of Allah be upon him', is written after the name of the Holy Prophet Muhammad[saw].

as   *Alaihis-salaam/ Alaihas-salaam,* meaning 'May peace be on him/her', is written after the names of Prophets other than the Holy Prophet Muhammad[saw].

ra   *Radiyallaahu 'anhu/'anhaa/'anhum,* meaning 'May Allah be pleased with him/her/them', is written after the names of the Companions of the Holy Prophet Muhammad[saw] or of the Promised Messiah[as].

rta	*Rahmatullaah 'alaihi/'alaihaa/'alaihim,* meaning 'May Allah shower His mercy upon him/her/them', is written after the names of those deceased pious Muslims who are not Companions of the Holy Prophet Muhammad[saw] or of the Promised Messiah[as].

www.ingramcontent.com/pod-product-compliance
Lightning Source LLC
Chambersburg PA
CBHW071602080526
44588CB00010B/987